Homeric Responses

Homeric Responses

Gregory Nagy

 University of Texas Press, Austin

First edition, 2003

Requests for permission to reproduce material from this work should be sent to Permissions, University of Texas Press, Box 7819, Austin, TX 78713-7819.

⊗ The paper used in this book meets the minimum requirements of ANSI/NISO Z39.48-1992 (R1997) (Permanence of Paper).

Library of Congress Cataloging-in-Publication Data

Nagy, Gregory.
   Homeric responses / Gregory Nagy. — 1st ed.
     p.   cm.
Includes bibliographical references (p.   ) and index.
    ISBN 0-292-70553-0 (cloth : alk. paper)
— ISBN 0-292-70554-9 (pbk. : alk. paper)
    1. Homer—Technique. 2. Epic poetry, Greek—History and criticism—Theory, etc. 3. Oral tradition—Greece. 4. Oral-formulaic analysis. I. Title.
   PA4037.N347   2003
   883'.01—dc21

                        2003008792

Contents

Abbreviations

BA	*The Best of the Achaeans* = Nagy 1979
BA²	*The Best of the Achaeans,* 2d ed. (with new introduction) = Nagy 1999a
GM	*Greek Mythology and Poetics* = Nagy 1990b
HQ	*Homeric Questions* = Nagy 1996b
MHV	*The Making of Homeric Verse* = Parry 1971
PH	*Pindar's Homer* = Nagy 1990a
PP	*Poetry as Performance* = Nagy 1996a

Acknowledgments

I take this opportunity to express my gratitude to all who have given me advice about various parts of this book, especially to Egbert Bakker, Graeme Bird, Timothy Boyd, Jonathan Burgess, Miriam Carlisle, Erwin Cook, Olga Davidson, Stamatia Dova, Casey Dué, Mary Ebbott, David Elmer, Douglas Frame, Madeleine Goh, José González, Ryan Hackney, Albert Henrichs, Carolyn Higbie, Alexander Hollmann, Marianne Hopman, Thomas Jenkins, Olga Levaniouk, Kevin McGrath, Richard Martin, Leonard Muellner, Blaise Nagy, Corinne Pache, Timothy Power, Laura Slatkin, Jed Wyrick, and Dimitrios Yatromanolakis.

The index was prepared by Keith Harris and Garnetta Lewis, whom I thank for their valuable work.

I dedicate this book to my son, László, with deep gratitude for his cheerful support.

Prologue

Homeric Responses builds on two earlier books, *Homeric Questions* (1996) and *Poetry as Performance: Homer and Beyond* (1996), which dealt with respectively earlier and later phases in the evolution of Homeric poetry. By Homeric poetry I mean the poetic system underlying the poetic texts that we know as the *Iliad* and the *Odyssey*. "Homer" is used throughout this book as a cover term for the *Iliad* and *Odyssey* combined.[1] This terminology follows that of Aristotle (*Poetics* 23.1459b1–7), who thought of Homer as the author of the *Iliad* and *Odyssey* to the exclusion of the so-called Epic Cycle.[2] In comparison with *Homeric Questions* and *Poetry as Performance,* the present book deals with a wider range of questions about Homeric poetry as poetry. It attempts to convey, however briefly, the essence of Homeric poetry in the fullness of its complexities. Still, most of the book can be read without specialized background in Homeric or even in Classical studies. Further, *Homeric Responses* does not require a reading of those two other books as general background.[3] Rather, it can serve as an introduction.[4] In addition, it can serve as an introduction to two even earlier books, *Pindar's Homer: The Lyric Possession of an Epic Past* (1990) and *The Best of the Achaeans* (1979; new ed. 1999).[5]

---

1. When I say "Homer," I intend it as a metonym for Homeric poetry. By "metonym" here I mean, as a working definition, the expression of meaning by way of *connection*—as opposed to "metaphor," by which I mean the expression of meaning by way of *substitution*. For an introduction to the poetics of Homeric and Hesiodic metonymy, see Muellner 1996. See also Martin 2000 on Homeric framing, juxtaposition, and *mise en abyme*.

2. *HQ* 38.

3. Still, I could never have written this book without first having rethought my way through *HQ* and *PP*. The extensive cross-references to these two earlier books in the footnotes here reflect that fact. These cross-references, regularly placed at the beginning of footnotes, are not meant to be seen as markers of final formulations. Rather, they point to earlier pathways of inquiry that have led to formulations found in the present book.

4. Although *HQ* covers the earlier phases of the Homeric tradition and *PP* the later, *HQ* is marked 1996b in the bibliography because it was published several months after *PP*, which is marked 1996a. *HQ* cross-refers extensively to *PP*, while the original *PP* has no direct cross-references to *HQ* as a book version, only to earlier versions published as separate articles (Nagy 1992a, 1992b, 1995a).

5. In *BA²* (= Nagy 1999a), the new edition of *BA* (= Nagy 1979), I incorporate changes prompted by important new research. See, for example, *BA²* 380, with reference to the dissertation of Wilson

Most of this book comes from work I have already published in a variety of far-flung settings. Some parts were commissioned for various projects distinct from my own. Most other parts, however, were originally conceived as ultimate components of the present book. What unites all the parts is a sustained interest in Homeric poetry as a unified poetic system.

In pursuing this interest, I invoke a dictum extrapolated from the work of Aristarchus, the most distinguished textual critic of Homeric poetry in the ancient world (middle of the second century B.C.E.): *Homēron ex Homērou saphēnizein*, 'clarify Homer by way of Homer'.[6] The clarifications provided by Homeric poetry itself are the unifying principle behind *Homeric Responses*.

My translation of the Aristarchean concept of *saphēnizein* as 'clarify' is pertinent to a celebrated metaphor applied to Aristarchus in the ancient world: Panaetius of Rhodes, an exponent of Stoic thinking, compared Aristarchus to a *mantis* 'seer', for his power to understand the *dianoia* 'meaning' of poetry (Athenaeus 14.634c).[7] The "clarification" of the critic is being equated metaphorically with the clairvoyance of the seer.

In this light, the expression *Homēron ex Homērou saphēnizein* 'clarify Homer by way of Homer' can be taken further. Aristarchus is oracular, that is, mantic like a seer, in clarifying the meaning of Homer because Homer himself is oracular in clarifying his own meaning. But how can we imagine Homer as oracular in his own right? Is it because his meaning is made clear by his critics? No, it is because he makes his own meaning clear to them. In the language of Homeric poetry, a seer has the power to clarify meaning. Just as the generic seer knows *sapha* 'clearly' the meaning of an omen, as we see later when we take a close look at relevant passages in the *Iliad* (such as 12.228–229), so also Homer seems to know that meaning—as well as all the meanings of all things considered in the overall poetry.

The metaphor of clairvoyance can be taken even further. My translation of *Homēron ex Homērou saphēnizein* as 'clarify Homer by way of Homer' is pertinent to the title of this book. *Homeric Responses* is, after all, a set of Homeric responses to questions, *Homeric* questions. Some of these Homeric "re-

---

1997 (see now also Wilson 2002). The present book tracks most of the changes summarized in *BA*² vii–xviii.

6. The wording comes from Porphyry *Homeric Questions* [*Iliad*] 297.16 (Schrader 1890); see also Scholia D to *Iliad* 5.385. On the Aristarchean provenance of the wording, see Porter 1992:70–74 (which effectively addresses the skepticism of Pfeiffer 1968:225–227).

7. Pfeiffer 1968:232; cf. *HQ* 3–4.

sponses" can be understood in the sense of the word *hupokrinesthai*, which means more than simply 'respond to a question' in Homeric usage. As we see in Chapter 1, this word conveys the idea of oracular response, that is, of responding in the same way as a *mantis* or 'seer' would respond to a question about an omen. Moreover, this word conveys the idea of responding, responsiveness, *in performance*.

There are also other kinds of "responses" offered by Homeric poetry. This poetry not only lays claim to a meaning made absolute by oracular authority, it also leaves room for meanings that are relativized. As we see in Chapter 4, even the overall meaning of Homeric poetry remains in question, depending on an audience imagined as ever different, ever changing.

This act of imagining a Homeric audience happens in a world of verbal art pretending to be visual art, the world as pictured on the Shield of Achilles in *Iliad* 18. Inside this world of pictures on the Shield, Homeric poetry makes room for the world outside itself, reaching beyond its own heroic frame of time. In the world of the Shield, Homeric poetry looks at other worlds in its own future, the era of the polis or city-state and, virtually, even beyond. The art of the Shield, which is Homeric art, envisions an ever-expanding outer circle of listeners. This vision conveys, again, the idea of responding, responsiveness, *in performance*.

The "responses" of *Homeric Responses* have to do primarily with the responsiveness of poetry *in performance* and even *as performance*. In other words, they have to do with the traditions of oral poetry, as described by Albert Lord in *The Singer of Tales*.[8]

When oral poetry is being performed, it responds to the occasion of performance. Such responsiveness is comparable to that of a seer, since the poetry provides potential answers to questions raised in the process of its performance. The actual responses, however, are decided not only by the seer-like authority of poets. The ultimate decision is left up to the audience at large, that ever-expanding outermost circle of listeners pictured on the Shield of Achilles. The responsiveness of Homeric poetry is mediated by whoever performs for such a generalized audience. Such a performer, in terms of Lord's model, is the singer of tales.

The driving idea of this book is that Homeric poetry, as a system grounded

---

8. Lord 1960; new ed., 2000.

in oral traditions, responds to questions raised not only by ancient Homeric audiences but even by today's readers of the Homeric texts. To that extent, *Homeric Responses* offers immediate answers to questions posed in my earlier work, *Homeric Questions*, as also to questions posed by critics of that work and other related works. The ultimate responses, however, must be sought— and found—in the panorama of oral poetic insights revealed by the Homeric texts themselves, echoing words once sung by singers of tales.

Introduction

Four Questions

Question 1: About Synchronic and Diachronic Perspectives

The terms "synchronic" and "diachronic" stem from a distinction established by a pioneer in the field of linguistics, Ferdinand de Saussure.[1] For Saussure, synchrony and diachrony designate respectively a current state of a language and a phase in its evolution.[2] I draw attention to Saussure's linking of "diachrony" and "evolution," a link that proves to be crucial for understanding the medium that is central to this book, Homeric poetry.[3]

Here I propose to add two restrictions to my use of "synchronic" and "diachronic." First, I apply these terms consistently from the standpoint of an outsider who is thinking about a given system, not from the standpoint of an insider who is thinking within that system.[4] Second, I use "diachronic" and "synchronic" not as synonyms for "historical" and "current," respectively. Diachrony refers to the potential for evolution *in a structure*. History is not restricted to phenomena that are structurally predictable.[5]

---

1. Saussure 1916:117.
2. Saussure, ibid.: "Est synchronique tout ce qui se rapporte à l'aspect statique de notre science, diachronique tout ce qui a trait aux évolutions. De même *synchronie* et *diachronie* désigneront respectivement un état de langue et une phase d'évolution."
3. The paragraph that just ended and the one that follows are an abridgment of my longer formulation in the new introduction to *BA*² (= Nagy 1999a), paragraphs 23–25. In the first edition of *BA* (= Nagy 1979), I had decided to avoid using the terms "synchronic" and "diachronic" altogether (though I had used them earlier in Nagy 1974, esp. pp. 20–21). Part of the reason for my return to Saussure's usage has to do with the remarks of Lord 1995:196–197 on the term "diachronic."
4. *PH* 4.
5. *PH* 21 n. 18, following Jacopin (1988:35–36), who adds: "Both synchrony and diachrony are abstractions extrapolated from a model of reality."

Question 2: About the Evolutionary Model

The evolutionary model was designed to account for the oral traditions that shaped Homeric poetry.[6] The main argument is straightforward: that the "making" of this poetry needs to be seen diachronically as well as synchronically. Here I return to Saussure's equation of "diachronic" with "evolutionary" perspectives.

In terms of an evolutionary model, there were at least five distinct consecutive periods of Homeric oral/written transmission—"Five Ages of Homer," as it were—with each period showing progressively less fluidity and more rigidity:[7]

1. A relatively most fluid period, with no written texts, extending from the early second millennium B.C.E. into the middle of the eighth century;

2. A more formative or "pan-Hellenic" period, still with no written texts, from the middle of the eighth century B.C.E. to the middle of the sixth;[8]

3. A definitive period, centralized in Athens, with potential texts in the sense of *transcripts,* at any or several points from the middle of the sixth century B.C.E. to the later part of the fourth; this period starts with the reform of Homeric performance traditions in Athens during the regime of the Peisistratidai;[9]

4. A standardizing period, with texts in the sense of transcripts or even *scripts,* from the later part of the fourth century to the middle of the second; this period starts with the reform of Homeric performance traditions in Athens during the regime of Demetrius of Phalerum, which lasted from 317 to 307 B.C.E.;[10]

---

6. See the new introduction to *BA²*, with special reference to *HQ* ch. 2, "An Evolutionary Model for the Making of Homeric Poetry," pp. 29–63. For an archaeologist's view of the evolutionary model, see Sherratt 1990, esp. pp. 817–821. For an early version of my model, see Nagy 1974:11. Cf. also Seaford 1994, esp. p. 144; Bakker 1997:21–22; Lowenstam 1997:58–67.

7. The scheme that follows is based on the outline in *HQ* 41–42, with details in *HQ* ch. 3; also in *PP* 110, with details in *PP* ch. 5–ch. 7. I originally used the term "Ages of Homer" as a tribute to Emily Vermeule (Nagy 1995a). The *HQ* and *PP* discussions, as I have just cited them, emphasize respectively the earlier and later phases of my evolutionary model.

8. For this period, I do not insist on the absence of texts; my point is simply that there is no compelling evidence for the existence of Homeric texts at such an early date. Cf. *HQ* 31–32. In a new project, I plan to rework my definition of "period 2" in the light of a forthcoming work by Douglas Frame on the Ionian cultural contexts of epic performance traditions.

9. *HQ* ch. 3; cf. *PP* 69–71.

10. *PP* 153–186.

5. The relatively most rigid period, with texts as *scripture,* from the middle of the second century onward; this period starts with the completion of Aristarchus's editorial work on the Homeric texts, not long after 150 B.C.E. or so, which is a date that also marks the general disappearance of the so-called eccentric papyri.[11]

The point of reference in setting up a scheme of five periods of Homeric transmission is the dimension of *performance,* not of *text.* Keeping in mind this dimension, I have developed special working definitions for the otherwise purely textual terms "transcript," "script," and "scripture," as assigned to the third, fourth, and fifth periods, respectively.[12] By *transcript* I mean the broadest possible category of written text: a transcript can be a record of performance, even an aid for performance, but not the equivalent of performance.[13] We must distinguish a transcript from an inscription, which can traditionally refer to itself in the archaic period as just that, an equivalent of performance.[14] As for *script,* I mean a narrower category, where the written text is a prerequisite for performance.[15] By *scripture* I mean the narrowest category of them all, where the written text need not even presuppose performance.[16]

A further distinction must be made between transcript and script. A transcript merely records a given performance and has no direct bearing on the traditions of performance. A script, on the other hand, controls the performance, making it uniform and keeping it from becoming multiform.

The distinction I have just made leaves room for the historical possibility of multiform "transcripts" stemming from multiple recurring performances of Homeric poetry. In other projects, I have explored this possibility in some depth, concentrating on allusions made by Plato to the performances of Homeric poetry by *rhapsōidoi* 'rhapsodes' at the Athenian festival of the Panathenaia.[17]

---

11. *PP* 107–152, 187–206.
12. *PP* 112.
13. *HQ* 34–36, 65–69.
14. *HQ* 34–36, with bibliography.
15. *PP* 153–186, *HQ* 32–34.
16. *PP* 187–206.
17. Nagy 1999c, 2000b, 2001b; book version: Nagy 2002a.

Question 3: About Dictation Models

Dictation models[18] are linked to the Homeric research of Milman Parry and Albert Lord.[19] They converge on the unifying idea of an original Homeric text dictated by Homer himself. Such an idea has been described as "the theory of the dictated text, a keystone in the Parry-Lord model."[20] There is no single theory, however, of a dictated Homer text. There are, rather, many such theories.[21]

No theory about Homeric dictation can be called a "keystone in the Parry-Lord model." Even the most persuasive of all the dictation theories, the original formulation of Albert Lord himself, was not a "keystone" of his model of oral traditional composition. Rather, it was more of a *parergon*.[22] As for Milman Parry, he never formulated a dictation theory.[23]

My own evolutionary model for the making of Homeric poetry is not at odds with dictation models per se.[24] I need to stress that I oppose not the idea of dictation but the application of this idea to various models posited by various scholars. In principle, my own model explicitly allows for a variety of historical contexts in which dictation could indeed have taken place, resulting in "a transcript, or a variety of transcripts, at various possible stages of the performance tradition of Homer."[25]

Since Lord rigorously avoided any speculation about any unique occasion for Homeric dictation, I do not disagree with his model. On the other hand, I do indeed disagree, in varying degrees, with others who posit various mutually irreconcilable dictation models.[26] My disagreement with one such

---

18. The original version of this section is Nagy 1997b, written in response to a review by Powell (1997) of *PP* (Nagy 1996a).

19. The central works are [M.] Parry *MHV* and Lord 1960, 1991, 1995.

20. See Powell 1997 (no pagination).

21. For example: Janko 1982:191; Jensen 1980:92; West 1990:34; Powell 1991:221–237.

22. The original theory appeared in an article, Lord 1953, which was later reprinted in Lord 1991 (pp. 3–48, with an appendix), a book published in the "Mythology and Poetics" series that I have edited.

23. For elaboration on this point, see below, Chapter 3.

24. The first formal version of my evolutionary model was published in a Festschrift for Albert Lord (Nagy 1981). For an earlier informal version, see Nagy 1974:11. See also in general above, "Question 2."

25. *HQ* 100.

26. See again Janko 1982:191; Jensen 1980:92; West 1990:34; Powell 1991:221–237.

model in particular, that of Janko, will be elaborated in Chapter 3.[27] For the moment, however, I confine myself to addressing a central assumption underlying another of these models.[28]

Here is the formulation of this assumption: "The monumental labor and expense required to record the *Iliad* and *Odyssey* ensure for most Homerists that the poems were recorded a single time, that there was an original text. What is the problem with such an assumption?"[29] The problem is this: as soon as dictation takes place, in terms of such an assumption, Homeric poetry becomes an Ur-text, and it can only be disseminated as a text.[30]

In terms of such an assumption, any performance of the Homeric poems, once they were dictated, was merely a matter of memorizing the dictated text. Such a model was rejected by Lord in formulating his own dictation theory.[31] Here are Lord's own words: "The singer has no need of a mnemonic device in a manner of singing that was designed to fill his needs without such written aids. A mnemonic device implies a fixed text to be memorized, a concept unknown to the oral poet."[32] Lord adds: "A written text would be useful to the reciter or rhapsode of a later period who is no longer an oral poet, but simply a mouthpiece."[33]

It is clear, then, that Lord associates the idea of a fixed text only with rhapsodes "of a later period." In terms of my evolutionary model, such a stage of evolution can be located at period 4 in my posited five-period scheme, which I date from the end of the fourth to the middle of the second century B.C.E.[34]

By contrast, according to the dictation model that we are now considering, a fixed text for performances of Homeric poetry must go all the way back to 800 B.C.E. or thereabouts. With this early dating of Homer, it becomes easier for this dictation theory to detach Homeric poetry from the rest of Greek literature: "Aristocrats, who learned how to decipher texts that began as oral poetry, discovered how to create, in writing, new forms of poetry, lyric

---

27. See also *HQ* 31–34, 36–37, 100.
28. Powell 1991: 221–237 (his chapter title is "Conclusions from Probability: How the *Iliad* and the *Odyssey* were written down") and 1997.
29. Powell 1997.
30. Powell 1991: 232–233.
31. Lord 1953 = 1991: 44; see further in *HQ* 32–34.
32. Lord 1991: 44.
33. Ibid.
34. *PP* 110; cf. *HQ* 42. See "Question 2" above.

and choral song (how do you train a chorus without a written text?); Sappho and Euripides composed for reperformance from a written prompt in just this way."[35]

To assume that "new" forms of poetry like lyric and choral song were "discovered" through the technology of writing is to ignore the history and prehistory of ancient Greek song culture.[36] Albert Lord's model of composition-in-performance applies not only to epic but also to lyric traditions.[37]

A related assumption is this: "An oral poem ceases to be an oral poem when it becomes a text."[38] I disagree. Turning an "oral poem" into a text does not by itself stop the oral *tradition* that created the "oral poem."[39] The oral traditions of composition-in-performance can be independent of a writing technology that turns compositions into texts.[40] This fundamental insight is evident throughout Albert Lord's last book, *The Singer Resumes the Tale*.[41] It is supported by a wealth of comparative evidence drawn from a variety of historical contexts.[42]

Further, in the case of a complex performative form like Attic tragedy, the written text of the composition can indeed serve as a script for performances, but those performances are rooted in earlier traditions of composition-in-performance. My evolutionary model does not rule out the concept of "script" in performative traditions.[43]

The concept of "script" does not depend, however, on the assumption that there is "an essential difference between the singer who composed in performance (the *aoidos*) and the reciter (the *rhapsōidos*), who memorized a written text for public reperformance."[44] There is no evidence for making such a sharp distinction, at any given historical moment, between *aoidos* and *rhapsōidos*. It would be more realistic to say that these two words represent relatively earlier and later stages in the prehistory and history of performance

---

35. Powell 1997.
36. Cf. [M.] Parry *MHV* [1932]:347–361.
37. Lord 1995:22–68.
38. Powell 1997.
39. *PP* 26–27.
40. Ibid.
41. Lord 1995, esp. chs. 1, 8, and 10.
42. Ibid.
43. See *HQ* 34–43. For more on the semiotics of "writing" as "composition," see "Question 4" below.
44. Powell 1997.

traditions. Only to that extent is it possible to make distinctions in form and function, over time, between *aoidos* 'singer' and *rhapsōidos* 'rhapsode'.[45]

The reconstruction of these distinctions is a far cry, however, from a blanket assumption of an "essential difference" between *aoidos* and *rhapsōidos*. There are points of convergence as well as divergence between the two words, and my evolutionary model posits a historical continuum linking one to the other.

To think of the *rhapsōidos* merely as the "reciter" of the Homeric text, as if the portrayal of a figure like Ion in Plato's *Ion* could serve to define the meaning of *rhapsōidos* throughout time, is to lose historical perspective. It is to ignore evidence for changes in the form and the function of the rhapsode in the course of historical time.[46] The history of Homeric rhapsodes needs to be correlated with the history of Homeric performance itself as a progressive movement from fluidity to rigidity in an ongoing *historical* process of re-composition-in-performance.[47]

Before I leave this question, I need to correct the claim that I reject "the Parry-Lord model."[48] For the record, nowhere in my publications do I write that I oppose Lord's theory, and I object to being portrayed as his opponent.[49] Since most of my scholarly life has been connected with Albert Lord, from my first year as a graduate student in 1962 all the way until the time of Lord's death in 1991, it is with the utmost seriousness that I view the importance of setting the record straight. I appeal for a correction, *sub specie aeternitatis*.[50]

Question 4: About Cross-References in Homer
The thesis here regarding Homeric cross-referencing is twofold.[51] First, I argue that the art of Homeric cross-referencing predates the writing down of

---

45. *PP* 59–78.
46. Cf. *HQ* 75–76, esp. n. 37, with bibliography. Clarke (1999:179) observes that my argumentation in *HQ*, as "a sustained hypothesis," can "offer a clear and manageable alternative to the now weary guess that transcripts of Homer's oral performances were handed down and used as secret cribs by generations of rhapsodes."
47. Ibid. See also *HQ* chs. 2–3, esp. pp. 111–112.
48. Powell 1997.
49. For a stance similar to Powell's, see Janko 1998c, whose rhetoric I confront in Chapter 3 below.
50. In the original version of this section, Nagy 1997b, I offered further comments that I omit here.
51. The original version of this section is Nagy 1998c. A drastically abbreviated version was folded into the new introduction to *BA*[2] (= Nagy 1999a).

the Homeric tradition. To put it another way, we need not assume that this art requires the pre-existence of a written Homeric text. Second, I argue that the mechanics and esthetics of Homeric cross-referencing are compatible with oral poetics.

Both arguments run into controversies. Some would assume that the very existence of cross-references in Homeric poetry justifies our thinking of this poetry as a product of textualization—or, let us call it *Verschriftlichung*.[52] In other words, some would assume that cross-referencing is a cognitive process that depends on or even stems from the technology of writing. In terms of my twofold thesis, this assumption is unjustified.

In general, I contend that such thinking is symptomatic of a widespread semantic trend in current everyday usage: when we say that Shakespeare "wrote" *Hamlet* or that Mozart "wrote" *The Magic Flute*, we slip into the mental habit of equating the mechanical process of writing with the mental process of composing.[53] The pervasive metaphor of substituting the concept of writing for the concept of composing stems from a built-in metonymy: We tend to connect the whole process of composition with what we ordinarily assume to be an essential part of that process—the part that involves writing. In classical Greek usage, by contrast, the metaphor of writing as composing is not nearly as pervasive: in the usage of Aristotle, for example, Homer is said to 'make' poetry, *poiein*, not 'write' it, *graphein*.[54]

My twofold thesis is linked to my evolutionary model for the making of Homeric poetry. Such a model can be applied to the major question at hand, that is, how is cross-referencing possible within an oral medium?

In earlier work, I offered the following formulation about cross-references in the earliest attested stages of Greek poetry: "When we are dealing with the traditional poetry of the Homeric (and Hesiodic) compositions, it is not justifiable to claim that a *passage* in any *text* can refer to another *passage* in another *text*."[55] I have added italics here to emphasize the inapplicability of

---

52. For the hermeneutics of the term *Verschriftlichung* 'textualization' as opposed to *Verschriftung* 'transcription', I turn to the engaging work of Oesterreicher 1993.

53. On the semiotics of writing and composing in general, I find Habinek 1998 particularly helpful.

54. See, for example, Aristotle *Poetics* 1451a25 ('Οδύσσειαν γὰρ ποιῶν οὐκ ἐποίησεν ἅπαντα ὅσα αὐτῷ συνέβη). The usage of *graphein* in referring to poetic composition is a relatively late phenomenon: see, for example, Pausanias 3.24.11, where he speaks of Homer as "writing" ("Ομηρος δὲ ἔγραψε μὲν τῆς ποιήσεως ἀρχόμενος ὡς 'Αχιλλεὺς; . . .) cf. also 8.29.2.

55. *BA* 40.

the word "text."[56] Granted, Homeric poetry must have eventually reached a point of textual fixation. Still, I apply this notion of textual fixation to oral traditions with an emphasis on gradual patterns of fixity in an ongoing process of recomposition in diffusion, and without presupposing that the actual composition of the "text" required the medium of writing.[57] My point is that cross-referencing does not presuppose a written text. In other words, I suggest that the notion of "cross-reference" is indeed workable in the study of oral poetics, provided we understand that any references to other traditions in any given composition/performance would have to be *diachronic* in nature.[58]

I draw attention to the use of the term "tradition" instead of "passage" in this formulation, revealing an intent to transcend the literal meaning of "textuality." By contrast, Pietro Pucci explicitly privileges the word "text," to such an extent that he even invokes the term "intertextuality" in the subtitle of a book on Homeric poetry.[59] Norman Austin, in a somewhat strained one-on-one contrast, has juxtaposed Pucci's approach with my own:

> For Pucci Homer is, beyond all considerations of oral composition, a text, or two texts (at least) reading and reflecting each other. For Nagy Homer is all tradition, and even to speak of the text is anachronism. The two scholars would seem diametrically opposed yet they have more in common than appears at first sight. Pucci's "text" is much more fluid than the text we associate with the written word, and Nagy's "tradition" is so conservative as to be itself a text, though a text without an author. Or rather, tradition itself is the author: Nagy refers to the Homeric poems as "the culmination of perhaps a thousand years of performer-audience interaction."[60] Pucci would seem more sympathetic to the idea of an individual author yet, given his concept of the fluidity of the texts reading each other, *it would be difficult to*

---

56. I disagree with Rutherford (1991–1993:42), who adds different italics to my formulation, thereby distorting it: "When we are dealing with the traditional poetry of the Homeric (and Hesiodic) compositions, it is not justifiable to claim that a passage in *any text can* refer to another passage in another text."

57. *PH* 53.

58. *PH* 53–54 n. 8, with examples from both Homeric and Hesiodic poetry. More on this point in what follows.

59. Pucci 1987 (see esp. p. 29 n. 30); see now also Pucci 1995.

60. Reference here to *BA* 15.

*locate any one moment when the individual poet, Homer himself, emerged
from the collective tradition.*[61]

I disagree with many aspects of this formulation, though I find it useful
for pursuing the topic at hand. I disagree especially with the presuppositions
at the end of the statement, as italicized. For similar reasons, I disagree even
more with this statement by J. S. Clay:

> I am not convinced that the Tradition, with a capital "T," can bear the
> heavy burden Nagy assigns to it. In and of itself, the appeal to Tradition
> smacks a little of questionable Romantic notions. While it may be
> able to expand or compress, modify or recombine older material, and
> even introduce novel motifs and conceptions, can the Tradition make
> cross-references where the precise context of the allusion carries the
> point? Or, finally, can the Tradition make jokes? Nagy himself speaks
> rather uncomfortably of the self-consciousness and self-reflectiveness
> of the Tradition.[62] But do such practices not require the existence of a
> closed tradition, one that has become fixed into a text?[63]

Clay follows up with this description of my method:

> But Nagy's general approach solves—or at least circumvents—a very
> sticky problem in Homeric studies. It permits us to accept all the ap-
> parent allusions and cross-references between the Homeric Epics with-
> out, however, demanding our acceptance of literal cross-references be-
> tween fixed texts. In other words, an apparent allusion in the *Odyssey*
> to an incident in the *Iliad* need not mean an allusion to the *Iliad* as we
> have it, but rather to that repertory of traditional motifs incorporated
> into our *Iliad*. In short, we can remain good Parryists and still allow
> ourselves to interpret the Homeric texts.[64]

---

61. Austin 1991:229; the italics are mine.

62. Clay (see next note) refers here to *BA* 20–21. I disagree with the idea that my pages there
reflect a discomfort with the concept of artistic self-consciousness in Homeric poetry. The point
was, and always has been, that such self-consciousness is different from what we find in written literature. Also, I call into question the vague reference to "questionable Romantic notions." On such
negative uses of the term "romantic" in polemics about the making of Homeric poetry, see *PH* 1–
2, where I point out that the negativity cuts both ways: those who assume an individual genius
called "Homer" can be just as naive as those who envision some kind of collective self-expression
by the ancient Greek "Volk."

63. Clay 1983:243. At this point, she refers to Pucci 1979:125.

64. Clay 1983:243.

What is missing in this description of my method is the most essential aspect: I insist on the need to find a poetic rationale, a teleology of meaning, in the process of cross-referring over time. In other words, there is a poetic system involved in the very act of Homeric cross-reference.

Further, I call into question the assumption that a "closed tradition" is to be equated automatically with "one that has become fixed into a text." I resist the absolutism inherent in such a description. It is as if we could find some kind of absolute distinction between "closure" and "open-endedness," corresponding to a surface distinction between written and oral traditions.

It seems to me that we could easily think of any given tradition, written or oral, as relatively "closed"—once we see it becoming internalized by the person who controls it. In other words, the concept of "closure" is relative to start with, not absolute. Any tradition can be considered "closed" to the extent that it becomes internalized by its practitioner. But the point is that the same tradition can be considered "open-ended" to the extent that it remains externalized for other potential practitioners. Even a relatively fixed tradition, notionally closed, cannot necessarily prevent successive reopenings of that same tradition by new practitioners.

We may expect to see varying degrees of closure and open-endedness in any tradition, oral as well as written. There are in fact extreme cases of relative closure in some living oral traditions as recorded by ethnographers.[65] Conversely, there are extreme cases of relative open-endedness in written traditions, where a notionally closed system of thinking becomes available for systematic reopenings. I propose to call this phenomenon the "Nostradamus effect."

I coin this term as a response to the meditations of Georges Dumézil on the oracular poetry of Michel de Nôtredame, better known as Nostradamus, who flourished in the sixteenth century c.e.[66] From the opaque verses of Nostradamus, Dumézil reconstructs, in broad strokes, the Classical *formation* of this mystical poet, which he compares with the *formation* of elite readers in the era of Louis XVI, toward the end of the eighteenth century.[67] This shared

65. See examples in *PH* 54–55, 80.

66. Dumézil 1984/1999. My first attempt at a formulation of the "Nostradamus effect" appeared in Nagy 1999d.

67. The focus of interest is on Nostradamus's vision of a blackfriar in gray, as quoted in the title of Dumézil's 1984 book ("*. . . Le moyne noir en gris dedans Varennes*"). In Nagy 1999d:vii, I drew attention to Dumézil's success in isolating a passage taken from the Roman historian Livy (first cen-

knowledge, as reconstructed by Dumézil from the verses of Nostradamus and from accounts of the final days of Louis XVI, produces an illusion of self-fulfilling prophecy. When a prophetic moment becomes internalized in the mind of Nostradamus and, two-and-a-half centuries later, in the mind of Louis XVI, the stage is set for an illusory effect to take hold: it now appears as if the opaque oracular verses of Nostradamus had prophesied what was actually going on inside the head of Louis XVI in the fatal moments that marked the cataclysmic end of royalty, and of a whole way of life, in revolutionary France.

We see at work here the communicative power of tradition. Even if a given tradition is closed to outsiders, it will remain open to insiders. Further, even if such a tradition is kept internalized by one person, it can become externalized by some other person who has also already internalized it. That is what I mean by the "Nostradamus effect."

By examining externalized forms of written tradition, as analyzed through comparative approaches, we can study empirically the opportunities for analogous reactions by different minds to analogous historical contingencies— reactions motivated by an analogous mental processing of tradition. In the case of Nostradamus and Louis XVI, for example, we see a convergence of two different minds in two different eras as they internalize—independent of each other—a shared written tradition, derived from an earlier era.[68] In such a situation, a comparative approach can trace the renewals of the earlier tradition in its externalized forms.

Such an illustration of independent internalizations by way of written tradition can help us appreciate all the more the relative open-endedness of oral traditions, which are generally not constrained by ideas of fixity suggested by the very existence of a written text.

Having outlined my overall approach to questions of "text," "tradition," and "cross-reference," I now offer a direct application, focusing on a specific passage taken from Homeric poetry. As a way of introducing the passage I have in mind, I quote what Austin has said about my approach, with specific reference to a theme signaled by this same passage. The reference concerns a quarrel between Odysseus and Achilles, as narrated briefly in *Odyssey* 8.72−83:

---

turies B.C.E. and C.E.) as a point of convergence in the readings of Nostradamus and, indirectly, of *literati* in the era of Louis XVI.

68. See especially Dumézil 1984:93−94.

Perhaps we should read the quarrel as representing the ramifying process whereby the same Mycenaean history *crystallized* into two separate epics *evolving* concurrently and synergistically, celebrating two kinds of hero, each noting and evaluating his rival's charisma as their reputations grew.[69]

Let us take a close look at this Homeric passage:

72 αὐτὰρ ἐπεὶ πόσιος καὶ ἐδητύος ἐξ ἔρον ἕντο.

73 Μοῦσ' ἄρ' ἀοιδὸν ἀνῆκεν ἀειδέμεναι κλέα ἀνδρῶν.

74 οἴμης. τῆς τότ' ἄρα κλέος οὐρανὸν εὐρὺν ἵκανε.

75 νεῖκος Ὀδυσσῆος καὶ Πηλεΐδεω Ἀχιλῆος.

76 ὥς ποτε δηρίσαντο θεῶν ἐν δαιτὶ θαλείῃ

77 ἐκπάγλοις ἐπέεσσιν. ἄναξ δ' ἀνδρῶν Ἀγαμέμνων

78 χαῖρε νόῳ. ὅ τ' ἄριστοι Ἀχαιῶν δηριόωντο.

79 ὡς γάρ οἱ χρείων μυθήσατο Φοῖβος Ἀπόλλων

80 Πυθοῖ ἐν ἡγαθέῃ. ὅθ' ὑπέρβη λάϊνον οὐδὸν

81 χρησόμενος. τότε γάρ ῥα κυλίνδετο πήματος ἀρχὴ

82 Τρωσί τε καὶ Δαναοῖσι Διὸς μεγάλου διὰ βουλάς.

83 ταῦτ' ἄρ' ἀοιδὸς ἄειδε περικλυτός· αὐτὰρ Ὀδυσσεὺς ...

72 But when they had their fill of drinking and eating,

73 The Muse impelled the singer to sing the glories (*kleos* plural) of men,

74 from a story-thread[70] that had at that time a glory (*kleos*) reaching the vast heavens:

75 the quarrel (*neikos*) of Odysseus and Achilles son of Peleus,

76 how they once upon a time (*pote*) fought at a sumptuous feast of the gods,

77 with terrible words, and the king of men, Agamemnon,

78 rejoiced in his mind that the best of the Achaeans were fighting.

79 For (*gar*) thus had oracular Phoebus Apollo prophesied to him,

69. Austin 1991: 233–234. At the end of this statement, he refers to my formulation in *BA* 21–25. On the semiotics of "crystallization," see *HQ* 109 and *PP* 108–109. With reference to Austin's wording, I distance myself from the notion of "history" in the expression "Mycenaean history," though I welcome the notion of a poetic tradition that can be traced back historically to the Mycenaean era.

70. On *oimē* in the sense of 'story-thread', see *PP* 63 n. 20; see also *PP* 63 n. 19 on the use of the genitive of this word here to mark the point of departure for the performance of the blind singer.

80   at holy Delphi, when he [Agamemnon] had crossed the stone
        threshold
81   to ask the oracle. For (*gar*) then (*tote*) it was that the beginning of
        pain (*pēma*) started rolling
82   upon both Trojans and Danaans, on account of the plans of
        great Zeus.
83   These things, then, the singer sang, whose fame is far and wide. But
        Odysseus . . .

Odyssey 8.72–83

I see in these verses an Odyssean cross-reference to the Iliadic tradition.[71]
My focus is on the wording of verse 81, *tote gar* 'for then it was . . .', where the
gar 'for' refers back to the time of the *neikos* 'quarrel' at verse 75, not to the
time of Agamemnon's consultation of Apollo's oracle at verse 79.[72] The *pēma*
'pain', prophesied by Apollo, *kulindeto* 'started rolling' at the precise moment
when the *neikos* 'quarrel' got under way. The wording of verse 81, I must
stress, cross-refers not only to the mention of the quarrel at verse 75 but also
to the precise moment of that quarrel: "By virtue of cross-referring to *a specific
point in epic time,* the wording *tote gar* 'for then it was . . .' at verse 81 cross-
refers also to *a specific point in a notionally total and continuous narration extending into the current narrative.*"[73] What we see at work here is "the essential *notion,* inherent in oral poetic traditions, of a total and continuous narration, of

---

71. Cf. *BA* 22.
72. For a valuable analysis of the syntax that drives the wording of verse 81, see Pelliccia
1985:185–186 n. 18:

> Nagy . . . understood line 81 τότε γάρ ['for then it was . . .'] to refer back to the
> time of the νεῖκος ['quarrel'], with the γάρ ['for . . .'] clause [of verses 79–80]
> taken as an isolated parenthetical aside reporting events prior to the quarrel.
> R. Fowler [1983:125] called this "a shaky interpretation of Greek," and corrected
> it thus: "The second γάρ depends on χρησόμενος (for successive γάρ's in Ho-
> mer cf. J. D. Denniston [1954] p. 58); lines 81–82 thus imply that troubles are al-
> ready besetting Agamemnon, probably at Aulis."—But the matter is not so
> simple. Fowler is referring to Denniston's entry on "successions of γάρ clauses or
> sentences, each clause dependent on the previous one" (*loc. cit.*); he does not men-
> tion Denniston's entry six pages later (64f.) on "successive γάρ's [that] have the
> same reference," nor the comment within that entry (65): "We must distinguish
> from the above passages others in which the first γάρ clause is parenthetical, and
> the references in the two γάρ clauses are therefore not parallel" (citing *Od.*
> 20.30506 [*sic*]). The arguments from γάρ are therefore inconclusive.

73. *BA*² xvii; italics supplied.

which any given performance is but a part."[74] The *tote* 'then' of verse 81 is a precise cross-reference to the *pote* 'once upon a time' of verse 76.[75] The *tote* 'then' marks a "return to the time-frame introduced by the earlier temporal adverb [*pote*]."[76]

In terms of my argument, such a return to an earlier time-frame is a matter of performance, not just composition. That is, the cross-reference represented in this story-within-a-story is performative as well as compositional. To put it yet another way, the blind singer is here being represented as *cross-referring by way of performance*.

Precisely because the "return" to the time-frame is performative, it can work not only from the present to the past but also from the present to the future. As we shall see in Chapter 1, the prophecy of an event in the plot of Homeric narration can "repeat" in advance the wording of that given event. In the case of *Odyssey* 8.79–81, which signals the prophecy of Apollo about the future quarrel between Achilles and Odysseus, we can imagine a hypothetical performance where the prophecy becomes a retelling of the story already at the moment of the prophecy. In other words, the "return" to the time-frame of the quarrel can be previewed by "retelling" it in advance.

From an evolutionary point of view, the actual sequencing of themes in the oral poetics of composition-in-performance becomes a tradition in and

---

74. *BA*[2] xvii paragraph 30 n. 2. See also *HQ* 77–82. By italicizing *notion*, I am stressing that the continuity and the totality are merely notional, not necessarily "real" for the empirical observer on the outside looking in, as it were. For comparative evidence on notional totality, see Flueckiger 1996:133–134.

75. See again Pelliccia 1985:185–186 n. 18:

> It might further be argued against Nagy that τότε in 81 most naturally refers to what immediately precedes it; but in fact it can with equal ease refer back to ποτε ['once upon a time'] in 76; cf. [Hesiod] *Th.* 58–68, where between correlated ὅτε (58) and τότε (68) there intervenes a passage (63–67) whose time reference is completely different from that of the correlated clauses: τότε here serves (as per Nagy it does in *Od.* 8.75–82) to dismiss the parentheses (corresponding to 79–81 in *Od.* 8) and *to return to the time-frame introduced by the earlier temporal adverb with which it is correlated.* This point has been repeatedly misconstrued by W. J. Verdenius [1972] 225–60; 247 esp.

Italics mine. Pelliccia (ibid.) adduces further examples, quoting from West 1985:129: "In *Th.* 68 τότε is resumptive, looking back to the account of the Muses' birth in 60 after the digression on their present-day activities." The scholia to *Odyssey* 8.75, we need to add, claim that the quarrel between Achilles and Odysseus took place *after* the killing of Hektor.

76. I am quoting again the italicized part of the formulation by Pelliccia in the preceding footnote.

of itself.[77] Such a tradition affects the phenomenon of cross-reference. Once the sequencing of Homeric "episodes" becomes a tradition in its own right, it stands to reason that any cross-referencing from one episode of the sequence to another will also become a tradition. It is from a diachronic as well as synchronic perspective that I find it useful to consider the phenomenon of Homeric cross-references, especially long-distance ones that happen to reach for hundreds or even thousands of verses: it is important to keep in mind that any such cross-reference that we admire in our two-dimensional text did not just happen one time in one performance, but presumably countless times in countless reperformances within the three-dimensional continuum of a specialized oral tradition. The resonances of Homeric cross-referencing must be appreciated within the larger context of a long history of repeated performances.[78]

From the standpoint of oral poetics in general, the referent of a reference is not restricted to the immediate context but extends to analogous contexts heard in previous performances.[79]

By contrast, some have interpreted the story-within-a-story at *Odyssey* 8.72–83 as an ad hoc invention, an *Augenblickserfindung*.[80] Bryan Hainsworth's commentary on the *Odyssey* accepts such an interpretation, further describing this story-within-a-story as an "allusion" that is "invented to meet the needs of the moment."[81] I disagree, contending that there is in fact no need to posit an ad hoc invention, that is, something that has never been narrated before. The "needs of the moment" are actually being met by a cross-reference to traditional themes that are part of the oral poetics of composition-in-performance.[82]

In Hainsworth's commentary, although he speaks of an "allusion" that is "invented" in *Odyssey* 8.72–83, we find that he accepts the traditionality of at least one of the themes in this Homeric passage:

> Yet the exaltation of Odysseus into an opponent of Achilles (he has no such stature in the *Iliad*) is not without significance. Achilles was the

---

77. *HQ* 77–82.
78. Most of this paragraph is excerpted from *HQ* 82.
79. *HQ* 82 n. 53; cf. Foley 1991 and my review in Nagy 1995b. For an important study of Homeric *Fernbeziehungen*, with conclusions different from mine, see Reichel 1994.
80. See Marg 1956:21. For a similar position, see Clay 1983:241–246.
81. Hainsworth 1988:351.
82. I disagree also with Clay 1983:243.

last and greatest of those heroes who solved their problems by excess of violence: Odysseus represents a newer idea (though we might see the germ of it in Odysseus' rational admonition of the impatient Achilles in *Il.* 19.155–183), probably congenial to many in the Homeric audience, the cool opportunist, valiant but prudent, and not ashamed to stoop to conquer.[83]

The problem is that this summary of a traditional theme makes that theme appear to be more a side-effect than a driving force of traditional Homeric narrative. I will not repeat here my arguments for the presence of this particular driving theme as revealed by the diction of the *Iliad* itself.[84] Instead, I turn to a related theme that happens to reveal more overt matches, *on the level of diction*, between the microcosm or micro-narrative of *Odyssey* 8.72–83 and the macrocosm or macro-narrative of the *Iliad*. This driving theme is made evident by the word *pēma* 'pain' in *Odyssey* 8.82, described as some colossal boulder that has just started rolling downward from the towering heights above, heading straight at the doomed Achaeans down below. This 'pain' signals an Iliadic theme, which can be summarized as follows: "Achilles is a *pēma* for the Trojans when he is at war and a *pēma* for the Achaeans both when he withdraws from war and when he dies." [85]

In our *Iliad*, this *pēma* 'pain' is realized in the death of Patroklos, which prefigures the "offstage" death of Achilles: [86]

’Αντίλοχ’ εἰ δ’ ἄγε δεῦρο διοτρεφὲς ὄφρα πύθηαι
λυγρῆς ἀγγελίης. ἣ μὴ ὤφελλε γενέσθαι.
ἤδη μὲν σὲ καὶ αὐτὸν ὀΐομαι εἰσορόωντα
γιγνώσκειν ὅτι πῆμα θεὸς Δαναοῖσι κυλίνδει.
νίκη δὲ Τρώων· πέφαται δ’ ὥριστος ’Αχαιῶν
Πάτροκλος. μεγάλη δὲ ποθὴ Δαναοῖσι τέτυκται.

---

83. Hainsworth 1988:351. At the end of this statement, he refers to Rüter 1969:247–254 (also to *BA* 42–58).

84. *BA* 45–49.

85. *BA* 64. This theme is linked to the name of Achilles, which can be explained morphologically as *Akhi-lāwos 'he who has *akhos* ["pain"] for the *laos* ["host of fighting men"]'. For more on the morphology and on the semantics of that morphology, see Nagy 1994a, where I develop arguments that anticipate the objections of Létoublon 1995:289–290. In a separate work, I criticize her general assumptions about the semantics of naming heroes.

86. *BA* 63.

Antilokhos! Come, so that you may learn
the ghastly news, which should never have happened.
I think that you already see, and that you realize,
that a god is letting roll a pain (*pēma*) upon the Danaans,
and that victory belongs to the Trojans; the best of the Achaeans has
    been killed,
Patroklos, that is; and a great loss has been inflicted on the Danaans.

Iliad 17.685–690

I find it essential to compare the words spoken by Menelaos[87] in referring to
any mortal who dares to fight Hektor *and thus undertake a confrontation with
Apollo himself:*

ὁππότ᾽ ἀνὴρ ἐθέλῃ πρὸς δαίμονα φωτὶ μάχεσθαι
ὅν κε θεὸς τιμᾷ, τάχα οἱ μέγα πῆμα κυλίσθη.

Whenever a man willingly, in defiance of a *daimōn*, fights a mortal
whom a god honors, surely a great pain (*pēma*) rolls down upon him.

Iliad 17.98–99

Patroklos had dared to confront Apollo, thus prefiguring Achilles, but
Menelaos dares not (*Iliad* 17.100–101).

On the basis of these two Iliadic passages, we can better appreciate the
significance of the first song of Demodokos in *Odyssey* 8.72–83 as a cross-
reference to a central Iliadic theme:

> Like some colossal boulder that has just broken loose from the heights
> above, the pain is now rolling precipitously and inexorably downward,
> heading straight at the doomed Iliadic warriors below. This powerful
> metaphor of epic doom, resonating through the fine-tuned words of
> Homeric song, evokes the grand images that link the first song of De-
> modokos with the ultimate song of Achilles, the *Iliad*.[88]

In the first song of Demodokos, *Odyssey* 8.72–83, we are looking at a
micro-narrative framed by the macro-narrative of the overall *Odyssey*. In this

---

87. "Agamemnon" has been corrected to "Menelaos" in *BA*² 63n.
88. *BA*² xviii.

micro-narrative, we see the oracular god Apollo engaged in the act of proph-
esying the macro-narrative of the *Iliad*—or, better, an *Iliad*. This micro-
Iliad, framed by the macro-*Odyssey*, is ominously encapsulated in a single
word, *pēma* 'pain', a superhuman force that threatens to crush the heroic an-
cestors of Hellenism (*Odyssey* 8.81–82).

Before leaving this question, I find it fitting to repeat an earlier formulation, most relevant to this book, about the first song of Demodokos:

> An *Iliad* composed by Demodokos would have been a poem with a
> structure more simple and more broad, with an Achilles who is even
> perhaps more crude than the ultimately refined hero that we see
> emerging at the end of our *Iliad*. I have little doubt that such an *Iliad*
> was indeed in the process of *evolving* when it was heard in the *Odyssey*
> tradition which *evolved* into our *Odyssey*. Demodokos had heard the
> *kleos* and passed it on in song.[89]

---

89. *BA* 65. I have added italics in order to highlight "evolving" and "evolved." This formulation is quoted by Clay (1983:242), but she omits the final sentence, through which I had meant to
convey the idea that the Iliadic cross-reference, as we have it, is a highly sophisticated artistic device. Clay's omission is symptomatic, I think, of her tendency to flatten out the diachronic dimension of my argumentation: see also Clay pp. 244–245, for her objections to my formulation of
"Monro's Law," quoted from *BA* 21. From this quotation, I repeat my own wording: "Or rather, it
may be a matter of *evolution* [emphasis added]. Perhaps it was part of the Odyssean tradition to
veer away from the Iliadic." One last time, I stress the diachronic perspective of cross-reference.

 **Chapter 1**

Homeric Responses

In *Odyssey* 8.72–83, the first song of Demodokos, we see a link between the oracular clairvoyance of Apollo and the poetic composition of Homer. Such a link, where the god's prophecy is equated with the plot of the poet's narrative, is relevant to the word "responses" in my title, which is meant to capture the meaning of the ancient Greek word *hupokrinesthai* as we find it in the language of Homer. This word means more than simply "respond to a question." It conveys the basic idea of *responding by way of performing,* and this idea links Homeric poetry with the clairvoyant language of seers. Such language has its own poetics, which I propose to call "mantic" or "oracular" poetry.[1]

I begin with a seemingly straightforward Homeric context. In *Iliad* 7, we hear a heroic speaker, Diomedes, making a speech in response to a preceding speech, a message that was delivered by Idaios, herald of the Trojans, to the Achaeans. This preceding message of the Trojans is "quoted" by the Homeric narrative (7.385–397), and so, too, is the corresponding message that Diomedes speaks in response, on behalf of all the Achaeans (7.400–402). Then the leader of the Achaeans, Agamemnon, is "quoted" by the narrative as well: in his speech, he refers to the response of the Achaeans, as spoken by Diomedes; as Agamemnon says, the Achaeans are 'responding', *hupokrinontai*, to a message delivered from the Trojans (7.407). The Achaeans respond by virtue of the fact that the words of their response have been performed by Diomedes (7.400–402).[2] Further, these words have been

---

An earlier and shorter version of this chapter is Nagy 2002b.

1. Cf. Koller 1957 on a basic insight: that the prehistory of oracular discourse in early Greek civilization is relevant to the prehistory of the word *hupokrinesthai*. (His article also provides a bibliography of earlier research on *hupokrinesthai* and its derivatives.)

2. For analogous attestations of *hupokrinesthai*, see *Odyssey* 2.111 and *Homeric Hymn to Apollo*

performed by virtue of the fact that they are being "quoted" by Homeric performance.[3]

Each time the *Iliad* was performed, over the many centuries of Homeric performance traditions, let us imagine how a given audience would have heard these words of the Achaeans' response, such as we have them in *Iliad* 7.400–402. For each new audience, it is notionally the exact same response all over again, because the original words of the original hero are supposedly being "quoted." These words of response would be imagined to be the "same" each time, I argue, not because they are written down—and to that extent my use of the word "quoted" is imprecise—but simply because they are performed. In terms of performance, the original words of a Homeric response are being spoken by the original speaker—in this case, by the hero Diomedes. The mentality of "quotation" is basically performative. What matters ultimately, as we shall see, is the actual performativity or "quotability" of *hupokrinesthai* in its Homeric contexts. Having made clear that I use "quotation" in a performative sense, I hereafter omit quotation marks when I use the word with reference to Homeric contexts.

The notional "sameness" of a Homeric response on each occasion when Homeric poetry is being performed is part of an overall mentality of unchangeability in Homeric performance itself. Such a mentality, I am arguing, is revealed by the Homeric contexts of *hupokrinesthai*. In other words, Homeric poetry presents itself as the same thing each time it is performed, just as the words of heroes (and gods) that are quoted by the poetry are imagined to be the exact same words on each occasion of each new performance.

I hasten to add a clarification: such a built-in mentality, operating on the idea that every successive performance of Homeric poetry is supposedly the same, cannot be taken literally to mean that this poetry had in fact achieved some kind of permanent fixity. A similar mentality can be found in many different kinds of oral tradition in general. Claims of "sameness" by a given oral tradition, where each performance is notionally the same thing as each previous performance, are easily contradicted by empirical observation. The evidence collected from a wide variety of living oral traditions makes it clear that

---

171. In the *Hymn to Apollo,* the quoted words of response, verses 172–174, are a description of "Homer"—as quoted by "Homer" himself: see *PH* 376.

3. The "quoting" of words in Homeric poetry is equivalent to performing the "quotation": see Nagy 2002a: 21–23 with reference to Martin 1989, esp. his p. 117.

the process of recomposition-in-performance results in various degrees of change during various phases in the evolution of these traditions. But the point is that the actual mentality of "sameness" is itself an empirical fact in its own right.[4]

Having noted this clarification, we are ready to survey some additional Homeric contexts of *hupokrinesthai*. Taken together, these contexts show that Homeric poetry views itself as a performance medium. Further, they show that this poetry has close links to another kind of performance medium, "mantic" or "oracular" poetry. In other words, Homeric poetry equates its own performance with that of a seer or *mantis* who performs oracular poetry in responding to questions about omens.

My first example of such an equation is *Iliad* 12.228, describing a hypothetical situation where *hupokrinaito* (ὑποκρίναιτο), meaning 'he would respond', has as its subject *theopropos* 'seer'. The speaker is the hero Polydamas, a comrade of Hektor, and he has just interpreted a *teras* 'omen' (12.209): it is the vision of an eagle that drops a snake in mid-flight. This omen is quoted directly by the words of Homeric narrative at 12.200–209. Then the meaning of these poetic words is interpreted by the likewise poetic words of the hero Polydamas at 12.210–229. The hero is quoted as saying, at the conclusion of his words, that these same words of interpretation could be matched by the words of interpretation spoken by a hypothetical seer (12.228–229). In other words, what the hero performs in the *Iliad* corresponds to what a *theopropos* 'seer' would perform if he responded to the same vision that has just been narrated by the *Iliad*.

A far more complex example of *hupokrinesthai* is *Odyssey* 19.535, where Penelope challenges Odysseus to respond to the omen of her dream about the killing of the geese in her courtyard by an eagle that swoops down on them: the verb *hupokrinesthai* is used here in the imperative, with the word for 'dream' in the accusative (ὄνειρον ὑπόκριναι). Primarily for this particular Homeric context of *hupokrinesthai*, the dictionary of Liddell and Scott offers the translation 'expound, interpret, explain'.[5]

Before we examine this context any further, let us have a look at an analogous context of *hupokrinesthai* at *Odyssey* 15.170, with reference to 'interpret-

---

4. *HQ* 40, with bibliography.
5. LSJ s.v.

ing' the ominous vision of a flying eagle that is holding a goose in its talons (15.160–165). I have elsewhere offered the following comment on the meaning of *hupokrinesthai* in this particular Homeric passage: "To *interpret* is really to formalize the speech-act that is radiating from the dream or omen."[6] The vision, as quoted directly by the Homeric narration in 15.160–165, confronts the eyewitness Menelaos with an implicit question: What is the meaning of this vision? The hero ponders how to 'respond', *hupokrinesthai*, at 15.170. Before Menelaos can speak, however, Helen anticipates him (15.171: ὑποφθα-μένη): she seizes the initiative and utters her own poetic words of response, quoted at 15.172–178. She describes herself as speaking the words of a *mantis* 'seer' (μαντεύσομαι, 15.172), since she is about to reveal how the course of narrated events will reach *telos* 'fulfillment' (ὡς τελέεσθαι ὀίω, 15.173). The words of this oracular performance by Helen, quoted at 15.172–178, give the meaning of the omen: just as the eagle seized the goose, so also Odysseus will deal with the suitors.

I should stress that the words of such an oracular performance are based on the actual vision of the given omen that is seen in "real life" or in a dream, and that this vision has to be performed first as a question—either by a character in the narration or simply by the narration itself—before its meaning can be performed as a response. Further, in the case of *Odyssey* 19.535, where Penelope challenges Odysseus to 'respond', *hupokrinesthai*, to the omen of her dream about the eagle and the geese, the dream *is* the omen.[7]

Once Penelope's vision of the dream about the omen of the eagle and the geese is expressed in her own performance (19.536–553), the ambiguities of its meaning are ready to be resolved in the counter-performance of a response. Surprisingly, the response in this case is already quoted within the dream, when the protagonist of the vision, the eagle, begins to speak and proceeds to interpret, within the dream, the dream itself (19.546–550). In effect, then, Penelope already has a response built into her dream, but she nevertheless challenges the disguised Odysseus to give his own response (19.535).

The rhetoric of Odysseus's response starts with a declaration that the meaning is so complex as to make any solution impossible. But then there follows a shift to a counter-declaration: that the meaning is in fact so simple that it is clearly visible. The solution, in other words, turns out to be self-evident.

---

6. *PH* 168 n. 95.
7. On the poetics of perception in quoted dreams, I value the insights of Murnaghan 1987:52.

Let us look at the precise wording. At *Odyssey* 19.555, Odysseus starts his response to Penelope by saying that there is no way to 'respond', *hupokrinesthai*, to her dream—and again the word for 'dream' is in the accusative (ὑποκρίνασθαι ὄνειρον). But the rhetoric is not yet complete: the verses that follow, 556–558, go on to contradict verse 555; as it turns out, there is no way to respond *if the speaker veers away from the words spoken by Odysseus in the dream*, that is, *if the words are changed*. But there is in fact one way—and only one way—to respond, namely, by repeating the words already quoted by Penelope herself in verses 546–553. For the meaning to be clarified, the quoted words would have to be quoted again, that is, performed. We see at work here the poetic mentality of unchangeability: once the words of response have been performed as a speech-act, they are ready to be quoted again as a fixed and unchangeable saying. I find it relevant that the figure of Odysseus is a master of changing the quotations of those he quotes, as he does in *Iliad* 9.[8]

In this passage of the *Odyssey*, of course, the time has not yet arrived for Odysseus to clarify his own identity, and so the ultimate clarification of the meaning of Penelope's dream is postponed. The point remains, though, that the clarification had depended on the quotation of the words of the eagle— words that had in fact already interpreted or mediated the meaning of the omen seen by Penelope in her dream.

In both these Odyssean passages about interpreting the meanings of omens about eagles and geese, as expressed by *hupokrinesthai*, it is essential to keep in mind that the omen, as quoted, is a *vision*. In the case of *Odyssey* 15.168, when Peisistratos asks Menelaos to respond to his question about the *teras* 'omen' of the eagle killing the goose, he says that it had been sent as an *epiphany* by a god: ἔφηνε θεὸς τέρας 'the god made as a vision the *teras*'. In the case of the omen that is Penelope's dream, her words make it clear that she is quoting what she actually *saw*. At *Odyssey* 19.537, Penelope describes herself in her dream as *seeing* her geese (εἰσορόωσα) at the very moment when the eagle is about to swoop down on them; at 19.567, her words describe dreams in general as things that one *sees* (ὅτε κέν τις ἴδηται).

The visual orientation of oracular poetry is evident in the ultimate *teras* 'omen' of the *Iliad*, the vision interpreted by the seer Calchas. The *Iliad* quotes

8. See further in Chapter 3 below, where I discuss Odysseus's rewording of the offer to Achilles by Agamemnon, as reformulated by Odysseus in his quoted speech from the Embassy Scene. Cf. Martin 1989:116–117, 123.

the seer himself at 2.324: ἡμῖν μὲν τόδ' ἔφηνε τέρας μέγα μητίετα Ζεύς 'Zeus the Planner <u>made as a vision</u> for me this great *teras*'. The *teras* 'omen', which is framed by the narrative of Odysseus (2.284–332)—which in turn is framed by the overall Homeric narrative—is the vision of a snake that first devours eight young birds and then the mother bird (2.303–320). The vision happened in the first year of the Trojan War, during a sacrifice on the occasion of the assembling of Achaean forces at Aulis (2.303). Next, we hear that Zeus, 'the god who <u>made the vision</u>' (θεὸς ὅς περ ἔφηνε, 2.318), proceeded to make this vision permanent and unchanging—by changing the snake into stone (2.319). In the words of Odysseus, the whole vision is a *sēma* (2.308), which we may interpret not only as a mental 'sign' but also as a concretized 'monument', a landmark.

Just as this petrified vision of the story of Ilion—and of the *Iliad* itself— is imagined as permanent and unchanging, so, too, is the *kleos* or poetic 'fame' that radiates from the words of the seer Calchas as directly quoted by Odysseus in *Iliad* 2.323–332. In the words of the seer himself, as we already saw at 2.324, ἡμῖν μὲν τόδ' ἔφηνε τέρας μέγα μητίετα Ζεύς 'Zeus the Planner <u>made as a vision</u> for me this great *teras*'. Then Calchas goes on to prophesy that the *kleos* of this *teras* will never perish:

ὄψιμον ὀψιτέλεστον, ὅου κλέος οὔποτ' ὀλεῖται

[. . . this *teras*], late in coming, late in coming to fulfillment (*telos*), and its *kleos* will never perish.

Iliad 2.325

That was then, at Aulis, in the first year of the Trojan War (*Iliad* 2.303). Now, as Odysseus is quoting back those same words of the seer, it is the ninth year at Troy (2.295). Calchas was saying, back then, in the words that are now being quoted by Odysseus (2.323–332), that the nine birds are the nine years that the Achaeans will spend at Troy, and that the citadel will be captured finally in the tenth year. After Odysseus quotes these words of the seer, he adds: τὰ δὴ νῦν πάντα τελεῖται 'and they are now reaching their fulfillment (*telos*)' (2.330).

In the poetics of the *Iliad*, the expression ὅου κλέος οὔποτ' <u>ὀλεῖται</u> 'and its *kleos* will never <u>perish</u>' applies not only to the fame of the *teras* at 2.325 but also to the fame of the main hero of the *Iliad* itself. In the words of

Achilles, ὤλετό μοι κλέος ἐσθλόν 'my *kleos* will <u>perish</u>' (9.415), with the choice of a safe homecoming, *nostos*. The alternative is worded correspondingly: ὤλετο μέν μοι νόστος 'my *nostos* will <u>perish</u>' (9.413), with the choice of *kleos*. Ultimately, Achilles chooses *kleos*, which he prophesies will be permanent and unchanging: ἀτὰρ κλέος ἄφθιτον ἔσται 'but it will be a *kleos* unwilting' (9.413).[9] In other words, the epic of Achilles is its own self-fulfilling prophecy.

Conversely, the prophecy of the seer not only is fulfilled by the epic but also becomes the epic. The *kleos* of the vision interpreted by Calchas, described as permanent and unchanging, becomes coextensive with the *kleos* of the *Iliad*, which likewise describes itself as permanent and unchanging. Moreover, the *Iliad* prophesies—even at its very beginning—that its own ultimate *telos* 'fulfillment' will be the same thing as the irrevocable will of Zeus: Διὸς δ' ἐτελείετο βουλή 'and the will of Zeus was reaching fulfillment (*telos*)' (1.5). So also the ultimate *telos* 'fulfillment' of the prophecy of Calchas will happen only when the tale of Troy is ended, when Troy is finally destroyed: only then will the prophecy 'reach its *telos*': *teleitai* (2.330).

There is a similar coextensiveness between the plot of the *Odyssey* and the prophecy of Helen concerning the omen of the eagle that kills the goose—a vision that challenges Menelaos to ponder how to 'respond', *hupokrinesthai*, at 15.170. As we already saw, it is Helen who seizes the initiative instead, and she is the one who utters the poetic words of response, quoted at 15.172–178. Speaking as a *mantis* 'seer' (μαντεύσομαι, 15.172), she prophesies how the course of narrated events will reach *telos* 'fulfillment' (ὡς τελέεσθαι ὀίω, 15.173). The words of this oracular performance by Helen, quoted at 15.172–178, express the meaning of the omen, and this meaning is equated with the outcome of the overall plot of the *Odyssey:* just as the eagle kills the goose, so also Odysseus will kill the suitors as the narrative reaches its *telos*.

As we see from the precise wording of *Odyssey* 15.168, the meaning of the *Odyssey* is formulated as an explicit oracular response to an explicit question about the vision of an omen. When Peisistratos refers to the *teras* 'omen' of the eagle killing the goose, sent as an epiphany by a god, he asks Menelaos

---

9. *PH* 244–245. On the epithet *aphthiton* in *Iliad* 9.413, see Chapter 2 below (originally published as Nagy 2000d). There I stress that attributive and predicative usages of adjectives can be explained as syntactical variants within one formulaic system, from the standpoint of generative grammar. See also Volk 2002.

to respond to this question:

ἢ νῶϊν τόδ᾽ ἔφηνε θεὸς τέρας ἦε σοὶ αὐτῷ

Did the god make as a vision this *teras* for the two of us or for
yourself?

Odyssey 15.168

Menelaos ponders how to respond, *hupokrinesthai* (15.170), to this question, but he fails, since Helen anticipates him (15.171: ὑποφθαμένη). The response of Helen makes it clear that the meaning of the vision—and the plot
of the *Odyssey*—concerns the agenda of Telemachus, as supported by Peisistratos. This meaning of the *Odyssey* is intended not for Menelaos and
Helen, characters who are left over from the old world of the tale of Troy,
but rather for the characters of the new world of narrative as represented by
Telemachus and his companion Peisistratos.[10] Once again we see that the
plot of Homeric narrative is coefficient with the prophecies contained by the
narrative.[11]

Just as the poetic words of an oracular prophecy are expected to match exactly the realities of the future that is being prophesied, so also the poetic
words of Homeric narrative are expected to match exactly the realities of the
past. Since Homeric poetry figures itself as the fulfillment of the prophecies
made in its own past, it is coextensive with oracular poetry: just as oracular
poetry guarantees the future, Homeric poetry can guarantee the past. When
a hero says, as we have seen in *Iliad* 12.228, that his quoted words are the same
words that a *theopropos* 'seer' would have 'responded', *hupokrinesthai*, if he had
seen the same vision (ὧδε χ᾽ ὑποκρίναιτο θεοπρόπος), this quotation is os-
tensibly reinforcing not just the credibility but also the exactness of the Homeric wording.

Similarly, when Calchas speaks as a *theopropos* 'seer' in *Iliad* 2.322 (θεο-
προπέων), his words need to be remembered exactly and quoted back exactly—as they are at 2.323–333—because the realities will turn out to be
exactly the way he tells them. When the words of the seer's oracular poetry

---

10. On Telemachus as a representative of the "post-heroic" age, see Martin 1993.
11. On the involvement of the figure Peisistratos, as notional ancestor of the Peisistratidai of
Athens, in the teleology of Homeric narrative, see *HQ* 43 n. 58.

are quoted back exactly at 2.323–333, the quoting itself is a demonstration of the unchangeability of these poetic words. So Odysseus concludes after quoting the words τὰ δὴ νῦν πάντα τελεῖται 'these things, as I now see, are reaching their fulfillment [= verb *teleō*]' (2.330).[12]

The recurring sameness of Homeric quotations, as signaled by such oracular words as *hupokrinesthai* 'respond', corresponds to the recurring sameness of the given vision that calls for the question that calls for the answer. In the case of the words of Calchas as quoted back by the *Iliad* at 2.323–333, the sameness of the original vision that is being retold is concretized in the image of petrifaction: Zeus turns the snake into stone at the critical moment when it has just devoured the nine birds (2.319). In doing so, the same god who had made the original epiphany has now made the centerpiece of that epiphany into a permanent landmark:

τὸν μὲν ἀρίζηλον θῆκεν θεὸς ὅς περ ἔφηνε

And it [the snake] was made a radiant thing by the very god that
    had made it visible [as an epiphany].

Iliad 2.318

The petrified snake, like some splendid statue sculpted by natural forces, radiates a permanent vision matching the permanent words that give it meaning. Such words provide the permanent response to the question posed by the permanent vision. It is this kind of definitive response, I repeat, that we see conveyed by the word *hupokrinesthai*.

I have just used the simile of a statue because I see a similar mentality of unchangeability at work in the wording inscribed on a bronze statue dated to somewhere between 490 and 480 B.C.E.:

πασιν ισ' ανθροποι|ς hυποκ|ρινομαι hοστις ε[ρ|ο]ται : |
hος μ' ανεθεκ' ανδ|ρον· 'Αντι|φανες δεκατεν

---

12. The particle δή here has an "evidentiary" force ('Aha, now I see that . . .'); for more on this sense of δή, see Bakker 1997:74–80. As for the usage of *teleō* 'come to fulfillment' here at *Iliad* 2.330, we may compare *Odyssey* 19.547, where the talking eagle of Penelope's dream prophesies that this dream (*hupar*) will come to fulfillment—that it will be *tetelesmenon* (verb *teleō*).

I respond (*hupokrinomai*) the same things to all men, whoever asks me:
Who among men dedicated me?[13] Antiphanes did, as a tithe.[14]

CEG 286 [*IG* I³, 533]

The mentality of unchangeability, where the response to the question is always the exact same thing said in the exact same words, is signaled here again by the word *hupokrinesthai*. In this case, of course, it is also signaled by the fact that the response is written down in the inscription. The letters will not change, just as the words of oracular response will not change. Still, I shall now argue that the actual writing down of the words is not at all the cause of the mentality of unchangeability in this inscription, but simply an effect. So also with the word *hupokrinesthai:* I have been arguing all along that the usage of this word can be viewed as the effect, not the cause, of an overall mentality of unchangeability in oracular poetry and, by extension, in Homeric poetry.

Turning now to the inscription featuring the word *hupokrinesthai,* let us start with the obvious: the letters of this inscription give potential voice to the words of response. I say "potential" because the voice is not built into the inscription. In the mentality of early Greek poetic inscriptions, including this one, the reader who happens to read a given inscription has to lend his or her own voice by reading the letters aloud, so that these letters may then transmit the words that the inscribed object is saying.[15] The speaker is not the inscription itself, nor is it the actual writing in a more general sense. Rather, the speaker is the dedicated object, which (or "who") is conventionally marked as the "I" of the discourse. The words of this discourse are inherent in the dedicated object, and it is the actual vision of the object that leads to asking it any question in the first place: Who are you and why are you here? The response of the object—I am such-and-such an object and I have been dedicated by so-and-so—is likewise dependent on the vision, which had set the framework of the question in the first place. The dedicated object can always give the same answer because it always gets the same question, given shape by the unchangeability of the vision that radiates from the object.

---

13. On the use of a relative pronoun for an indirect question, cf. *PH* 221 n. 34.

14. I no longer agree with my translation as given in *HQ* 35 n. 25: now I take the genitive-plural construction 'among men' to go with "who," not with "Antiphanes."

15. Svenbro 1988:33–52 (= 1993:26–43), esp. pp. 36–38 (= 29–31); cf. also Day 1989.

In this case, then, the unchanging response is notionally spoken by the dedicated object, the statue, who is the "I" that responds to all the questions that come from all those who engage with the vision of the statue. To repeat, I concede that the mentality of unchangeability is reinforced by the writing down of these words. Still, ideologically, these words of response would stay the same even without writing, since they are predicated on the overall vision of the statue.

The mentality of this inscription has been compared to a celebrated passage in Plato *Phaedrus* 275d, where the figure of Socrates remarks that an author's writings will always 'signify' (*sēmainein*) the same thing each time you ask these writings a question.[16] The comparison is valid, to the extent that the writings of authors in books give a seemingly unchangeable response, much as the responses expressed by the word *hupokrinesthai* are notionally unchangeable. But there is also a fundamental difference: the "responses" of authors' writings, as described by Plato's wording here and elsewhere, are not expressed in terms of the word *hupokrinesthai*.[17] As I have argued from the contexts of *hupokrinesthai*, this word presupposes a response that is predicated on a specific question, which in turn is predicated on a specific vision. By contrast, the contexts evoked by Plato require no such predications.

In this light, let us take a second look at the notion expressed in Plato *Phaedrus* 275d, that an author's writing gives the same meaning each time you ask it to respond. This notion is actually linked with another notion, about the experience of vision: when you look at a painting, *zōgraphia*, and you ask it a question, its response is nothing but an august silence (275d). Such a mentality is quite different from the one conveyed by *hupokrinesthai*, where visualization can be translated directly into verbalization: the vision provides the question, which in turn provides the unchangeable response. When an oracle responds to a question about a vision, the unchangeability of that oracular re-

---

16. Svenbro 1988:36 (= 1993:28–29).

17. In his discussion of Plato *Phaedrus* 275d, Svenbro cites analogous passages in Plato *Protagoras* 329a (when you ask them a question, books have nothing to answer, *apokrinesthai* [not *hupokrinesthai*], nor any questions to ask), *Hippias Minor* 365c–d (not directly relevant to books per se: Socrates says that it is impossible to ask Homer what he really meant to say, so that Hippias should answer Socrates on Homer's behalf as well as on his own; cf. *Republic* 2.378d), *Laws* 12.968d–e (only tangentially relevant; no direct references to questions and answers), *Letters* 7.343a (on the idea of the *ametakinēton*, the 'unchangeable', in writings).

sponse is a sign of the vision's responsiveness. By contrast, Plato's notion of viewing a painting presupposes the notion of a vision's unresponsiveness to the viewer. In terms of these Platonic notions, when you ask a painting what it means, it cannot answer you, and so also when you ask a piece of writing what it means, it can only answer you with the words that you read in the writing.

For Plato, such a response is of course insufficient, since it may not suit the question. For Plato, a response from a book cannot foresee every question. In the case of archaic contexts expressed by *hupokrinesthai*, by contrast, a response suffices to the extent that it has been made—in performance—to suit a question about a vision. That is, such a response suffices so long as the meaning of the vision is made clear.

When we examine the contexts of *hupokrinesthai* in historicized accounts of oracular responses, as in the *History* of Herodotus, we can see even more clearly the importance of the vision, of the visualization of the vision, as the basis for verbalizing any given oracular response. For example, Croesus of Lydia knows that he has had a vision when he 'sees' (ἰδόντι) horses devouring snakes, and he recognizes this vision as a *teras* 'omen' (1.78.1); he therefore orders his *theopropoi* 'seers' to consult the oracular *exēgētai* 'interpreters' of Telmessus with the question, 'What does the omen (*teras*) mean (*sēmainein*)?' (τὸ θέλει σημαίνειν τὸ τέρας, 1.78.2). The *theopropoi*, once they get a response, do not have a chance to *apangellein* 'announce' it to Croesus, because in the meantime he has been defeated and captured by Cyrus (1.78.2). The content of the oracular response given by the interpreters of Telmessus is at this point quoted in indirect discourse, introduced by the expression 'these were the things they had recognized' (τάδε ἔγνωσαν, 1.78.3). The response makes clear the basic equation: that the snake is the same thing as an autochthonous native son, that is, Croesus the Lydian, while the horse is the same thing as an enemy newcomer, that is, Cyrus the Persian (1.78.3). Then, the content of the oracular response is concluded with the expression 'these were the things they had said in responding (*hupokrinesthai*)' (ταῦτα ὑπεκρίναντο, 1.78.3).

Here is another important example in Herodotus: Croesus sends messengers to the Oracle at Delphi, asking (εἰρωτᾶν/ἐπειρωτᾶν, 1.90.4), among other things, why the Oracle had encouraged Croesus to initiate war against Cyrus. The response is given by the chief priestess of the Oracle, the Pythia, and the content of this oracular response is quoted in indirect discourse

(1.91.1–5). At one point in the course of this response, it is made explicit by the Pythia that Croesus had 'asked' (ἐπείρεσθαι, picked up later by ἐπανειρόμενος, 1.91.4) his original question wrongly. At a later point, referring to a verse of oracular poetry that is actually quoted earlier by the narrative (1.55.2), the Pythia makes clear an essential equation, declaring explicitly that Cyrus is the same thing as the *hēmionos* 'mule' that had been visualized by the riddling verse of that earlier oracular response. Then, the content of the current response is concluded with the expression 'these were the things that the Pythia had said in responding (*hupokrinesthai*)' (ταῦτα μὲν ἡ Πυθίη ὑπεκρίνατο, 1.91.5). It is these words of response, ultimately, that the messengers of Croesus bring back to *apangellein* 'announce' to him.[18]

The visualization that is built into the verbalization of oracular responses must extend from the one who gives the response to the one who receives it. In the traditions of the Oracle at Delphi, a word that conventionally designates the recipient of the oracular response makes the idea of visualization explicit: it is *theōros*, meaning literally 'he who sees [root *hor*-] a vision (*thea*)', designating the messenger who is sent by his city to ask the question to which the Pythia will respond (Suda s.v. τὰ τρία; Theognis 805; Sophocles *Oedipus Tyrannus* 114).[19]

Such messengers can be *theopropoi* 'seers' in their own right, as we see from a story told by Herodotus about the consultation of the Delphic Oracle by the Athenians during the crisis of the Persian invasion (7.140–144). According to this story, the force of an oracular statement is not activated, the words do not become a completed speech-act, until they are performed before the audience for whom it was intended. Herodotus tells of Athenian emissaries who consulted the Delphic Oracle about their impending fate in the Persian War and who wrote down what the Oracle told them; having

---

18. Moving from Herodotus, we may note the usage of *hupokrinesthai* in Thucydides. At Thucydides 7.44.5, we read that the Athenians did not know how to respond, *hupokrinointo* (ὑποκρίνοιντο), to the *xunthēma* 'watchword' of the Syracusans. From 7.44.4, it becomes clear that both the Athenians and the Syracusans had their own watchwords, which were formulated in the form of *erōtēmata* 'questions'. To save your life, you had to have the right response (*hupokrinesthai*) to the right question. (The Oxford Classical Texts edition [1901+] of H. S. Jones simply prints the M manuscript reading ἀποκρίνοιντο, without indicating the *lectio difficilior* ὑποκρίνοιντο, as found in other manuscripts.) The Athenians, in the darkness, would keep asking, *erōtōntes*, their password, thereby making it *saphes* 'clear' for the enemy. The Syracusans were understanding, *epistamenoi*, the *xunthēma* of the Athenians, while the Athenians did not correspondingly (*homoiōs*) understand, *ēpistanto*, that of the Syracusans (7.44.5).

19. For further discussion, see *PH* 164–167.

written it down, they returned to Athens and ἀπήγγελλον ἐς τὸν δῆμον, 'announced (*apangellein*) it to the people' (7.142.1).[20]

In this narrative, the oracular poetry of the Delphic Oracle is delivered directly by the Pythia herself in hexameters; at one point, the narrative refers to her as the chief *mantis* 'seer' (7.141.2: ἡ πρόμαντις).[21] In other narratives about oracular responses, there may be an intermediary, the *prophētēs* (whence the English word "prophet"), who transforms the oracular words of the *mantis* 'seer' into formal poetry (Herodotus 8.135.3).[22]

There are many other variations in the usage of such words as *mantis*, *prophētēs*, and *theōros*, reflecting a variety of cultural differences in the traditions of oracular poetry.[23] Accordingly, we should not be surprised to find stories about disputes over the truth value of various historical instances of oracular poetry.[24] We see an example even in the story that we have just considered, concerning the consultation of the Delphic Oracle by the Athenians during the crisis of the Persian invasion (7.140–144): in this case, the responses of the Pythia, a set of oracular poems formulated in hexameter, provoke conflicts in interpreting the words of the Oracle, leading Themistocles to declare that the *khrēsmologoi* 'oracle-sayers' have not understood everything *orthōs* 'correctly' (7.143.1: οὗτος ὡνὴρ οὐκ ἔφη πᾶν ὀρθῶς τοὺς χρησμολόγους συμβάλλεσθαι).

What, then, is the word for what Themistocles is doing at the moment when he gives a different interpretation of the Oracle's words? Galen in his *Protrepticus* (13) describes Themistocles at this moment as engaged in the process of *hupokrinesthai;* in the idiom, the words of the oracle become the direct object (ὑποκρινομένου τὸν χρησμόν). That is, Themistocles is *interpreting* the oracle in the process of quoting the words, *performing* them all over again.

Here we confront a basic problem. How is the performance of Themistocles, as expressed by the word *hupokrinesthai*, different from that of the Pythia, as also expressed by *hupokrinesthai?* The mind of the priestess, as chief

---

20. *PH* 168.

21. Note, too, the context of *promantis* in Herodotus 6.66.2.

22. See further in *PH* 168 n. 95.

23. For a general discussion, see *PH* 164–169.

24. Of particular interest are stories suggesting that the Pythia was on various historical occasions "persuaded" to declare oracular pronouncements that were prejudiced in favor of special-interest groups: see, for example, Herodotus 6.66.3, 6.75.3 (cf. *PH* 163).

mantis, is notionally possessed by the god, inspired, at the time of her performance. Are we to say, by contrast, that Themistocles was not possessed at the time of his own performance? Here it is relevant to cite Plato's description of the *prophētēs* as an oracular poet who, unlike the *mantis,* performs without being possessed or inspired:

τοῦ δὲ μανέντος . . . οὐκ ἔργον τὰ φανέντα καὶ φωνηθέντα ὑφ' ἑαυτοῦ κρίνειν. . . . ὅθεν δὴ καὶ τὸ τῶν προφητῶν γένος ἐπὶ ταῖς ἐνθέοις μαντείαις κριτὰς ἐπικαθιστάναι νόμος· οὓς μάντεις αὐτοὺς ὀνομάζουσίν τινες. τὸ πᾶν ἠγνοηκότες ὅτι τῆς δι' αἰνιγμῶν οὗτοι φήμης καὶ φαντάσεως ὑποκριταί, καὶ οὔτι μάντεις, προφῆται δὲ μαντευομένων δικαιότατα ὀνομάζοιντ' ἄν.

But when some person is in a state of mental possession, . . . it is not that person's task to sort out (*krinein*) the visions that are made visible to him or the words that are voiced by him. . . . For this reason it is customary to appoint the class of *prophētai* as *kritai* [= 'those who sort out' = 'judges'] presiding over oracular utterances (*manteiai*) that had been made [by others] in the state of mental possession by the god. They [= the *prophētai*] are called by some, in ignorance, *manteis.* This is to ignore completely the fact that they [= the *prophētai*] are *hupokritai,* by ways of riddles (*ainigmoi*), of oracular utterance (*phēmē*) and oracular vision (*phantasis*). So they would be most accurately called the *prophētai* of things that are uttered by those who function as *manteis.*

Plato *Timaeus* 72a–b

We see here the agent noun of the verb *hupokrinesthai, hupokritēs,* in the sense of a performer who is no longer possessed, no longer inspired by the god. But we must keep in mind that the context here reflects Plato's own philosophical agenda, and that only in this context is the *prophētēs* assumed to be uninspired. In non-Platonic contexts, the *prophētēs,* too, is considered to be inspired (e.g., Pindar *Nemean* 1.60; Herodotus 3.37.2).[25] The distinction between *mantis* and *prophētēs* is not a question of being inspired or not inspired. Rather, it is a question of different degrees of formalization: whereas the words of a *mantis* may or may not be poetic, those of a *prophētēs* are pre-

---

25. *PH* 163–164.

dictably so. A salient example is Bacchylides *Epinician* 8.3, where the generic poet is the *prophētēs* of the Muse.[26]

As with *prophētēs*, so also with *hupokritēs*: it does not need to be taken in the sense of a performer who is no longer possessed, no longer inspired by the god. Plato's wording, as we have seen, describes *hupokritēs* as one who interprets, by way of performing, the utterance (*phēmē*) and the vision (*phantasis*) of a given oracle. There is no need to follow Plato, however, in assuming that such a *hupokritēs* must be disconnected from the visualization and the verbalization of the oracular vision. Just as the verb *hupokrinesthai* is predicated on the idea of a preexisting vision, so also the noun *hupokritēs*. In the case of *hupokrinesthai*, as we have seen, the idea of vision is evident from the word's conventional associations with such other words as *theōros*, meaning literally 'he who sees [root *hor-*] a vision (*thea*)'. In the case of *hupokritēs*, as we shall now see, the word is associated with *theatron* 'theater', meaning literally 'the vehicle for achieving vision (*thea*)'. In fact, *hupokrinesthai* and *hupokritēs* become the words for 'perform' and 'performer' in the language of Athenian State Theater.

I find it relevant and even essential to consider at this point the verb *hupokrinesthai* in the sense of 'perform in theater', with the object of performance in the accusative. A case in point is Demosthenes 19.246: τὴν Ἀντιγόνην Σοφοκλέους ὑποκέκριται as 'he has performed the *Antigone* of Sophocles'. The definition of *hupokrinesthai* in the dictionary of Liddell and Scott (LSJ s.v., B II) is suggestive: "*Speak in dialogue*, hence *play a part* on the stage, the part played being put in [the accusative]." By metonymy, the part can become the whole (as reflected in the italics that I used here for *Antigone*), so that the part being played stands for the whole play. We may compare such accusative constructions as τὸ δρᾶμ' . . . ὑπεκρίναντο 'they performed the drama' (again, Demosthenes 19.246). We may compare also ὑπεκρίνω plus accusative of the words being spoken (at Demosthenes 19.250). Another relevant example is Aristotle *Rhetoric* 3.1403b23: ὑπεκρίνοντο γὰρ αὐτοὶ τὰς τρα-γῳδίας οἱ ποιηταὶ τὸ πρῶτον 'in the beginning the poets themselves used to perform their tragedies'.[27]

Besides the verb *hupokrinesthai* in the contexts just surveyed, I find it just as essential to consider the noun *hupokritēs*, which is the standard word for

---

26. See further examples in *PH* 163.
27. Nagy 2002a:10.

'performer in theater', 'actor' (Plato *Republic* 2.373b, *Symposium* 194b, etc.). This word is used in parallel contexts with a word that refers to the performer of Homeric poetry, the *rhapsōidos* 'rhapsode', as in Plato *Ion* 532d7.[28]

The concept of the rhapsode is basic for understanding the central argumentation of this essay—and of this whole book. Just as the *rhapsōidos* performs Homer, so, too, the *hupokritēs* performs drama and other forms of poetry. Conversely, just as the *hupokritēs* acts out his given role in drama, so, too, the *rhapsōidos* acts out his given role as the master narrator of the Homeric *Iliad* and *Odyssey*.

When a rhapsode like Plato's Ion performs Homeric poetry, he is not only "quoting" the words of heroes and gods, thereby "acting" both their words and their personalities, he is also "quoting" the words of Homer, which are the narrative frame of heroic song. That is, the rhapsode is also "acting" both the words and the persona of Homer himself.[29]

Not only is the *hupokritēs* parallel to the *rhapsōidos*, "the term *hupokritēs*, normally used of the dramatic actor, could also be used of the rhapsode."[30] The performance of Homeric poetry by rhapsodes, just like the performance of dramatic poetry by actors, requires a responsive mentality, as conveyed by the word *hupokrinesthai*.

The connection between the meanings of *hupokritēs* and *rhapsōidos* is relevant to the collocation of *hupokrinesthai* and *hupolambanein*, as in Aristotle *Politics* 5.1310a10. Let us consider the definition for *hupolambanein* in the dictionary of Liddell and Scott: "In discourse, *take up* what is said, *interpret* or *understand* it in a certain way" (e.g., Plato *Republic* 1.338d).[31] In dramatized dialogue, *hupolambanein* marks the response of one speaker to the previous speaker: *ephē hupolabōn* 'he said in response' (e.g., Plato *Republic* 1.331d, etc.; Herodotus 1.11.5, 1.27.4, etc.). The noun *hupolēpsis*, derived from *hupolambanein*, is in fact a technical rhapsodic term ("Plato" *Hipparkhos* 228b–c).[32]

The dictionary definition of *hupolambanein* as 'interpret' calls for further comment. The very act of *performing* can be considered an act of *interpretation*, as we see from such modern usages as French *interpréter* in the sense of

28. Ibid.: 28.
29. *PP* 86, 220.
30. Murray 1996:110, referring to Koller (1957:104), who cites collocations of *hupokritēs* and *rhapsōidos* in Plato *Ion* 532d, 535e.
31. LSJ s.v.
32. Nagy 2002a:10–11.

'sing' or 'play' a given musical composition. In this light, let us consider the idea inherent in usages of *krinein*, from which the compound form *hupokrinesthai* is derived. This verb *krinein*, in the active voice, can be translated as 'interpret' when combined with the noun *opsis* 'vision' as its object (Herodotus 7.19.12) or with *enupnion* 'dream' as its object (Herodotus 1.120).[33] It is a question of interpreting-in-performance. The middle voice of *hupokrinomai* suggests that the performer is interpreting for himself as well as for others.[34] The basic idea of *hupokrinesthai*, then, is to see the real meaning of what others see, and to "quote" this vision for them.

Whereas the art of the rhapsode, as conveyed by the word *hupokrinesthai* and related forms, is associated with the idea of responsiveness, Plato seems to associate this art with the idea of unresponsiveness. We may consider in this regard another compound of *krinein*, that is, *anakrinein*, which means 'interrogate [judicially]', as in Thucydides 1.95. In Plato *Phaedrus* 277e, we read of *logoi* that are *rhapsōidoumenoi* 'performed rhapsodically' and are exempt from *anakrisis* 'interrogation' (οἱ ῥαψῳδούμενοι ἄνευ ἀνακρίσεως).

I come back to the central point, that the performance of Homeric poetry by rhapsodes requires a responsive mentality, as conveyed by the word *hupokrinesthai*. I repeat also a related point: that the framing words of Homer require the same responsive mentality as is required by the framed words of heroes and gods. The performance of Homer as a speaker mirrors the performances of the heroes and gods whose speeches he frames.[35] Homer as the framing narrator mirrors the poetic virtuosity of his framed epic characters, especially Achilles.[36] The responsive mentality of speakers in Homeric song extends ultimately to Homer himself, who becomes reenacted again and again in the traditions of rhapsodic performance.

---

33. Koller 1957:101.
34. Ibid.: 102.
35. This point is argued most effectively by Martin (1989; see esp. pp. 231–239).
36. Martin 1989:220–230.

Chapter 2

Homeric Rhapsodes and the Concept of Diachronic Skewing

Throughout this book, I maintain that the traditions of rhapsodic performance are essential for understanding the evolution of Homeric composition. Such an understanding, however, is impeded by various assumptions about rhapsodes as performers of Homer. Here I challenge some of those assumptions by reexamining the very concept of the *rhapsōidos* in terms of Homeric art. For such a reexamination, I invoke the concept of diachronic skewing.

The word "skewing" implies a slanted perspective, as if by way of squinting. The vision is distorted, with one side or direction unduly emphasized over another. The everyday usage of the contemporary English "skew" may imply a willful distortion of the truth, as in the expression "skewing the data," but my usage is not meant to imply *intentional* falsification.

Reconstructing ancient Greek song and poetry forward in time, I developed the concept of diachronic skewing in order to account for situations "where the medium refers to itself in terms of earlier stages of its own existence."[1] Focusing on oral poetic traditions of recomposition-in-performance as they evolved into the attested literary traditions of the Classical and Hellenistic periods, I contended that poetic self-references "may be diachronically valid without being synchronically true."[2]

The medium of Homeric poetry is replete with self-references by the medium to the medium, and it is in these self-references that we find the clearest examples of diachronic skewing. These examples center on rhapsodic traditions of performing Homer.

The original version of this essay is Nagy 2000d. (In that version, it is important to keep in mind that the word *attribut* in French refers to predicative rather than attributive uses of adjectives, whereas *épithète* refers to attributive uses.)

1. *PH* 394; cf. *HQ* 20 n. 27.
2. *PH* 21.

Right from the start, we need to confront the general nature of any reference, not just self-reference, in the various media of oral poetics. On the basis of my own cumulative work, I am convinced that any meaning by way of
any reference in oral poetics needs to be seen diachronically as well as synchronically: "Each occurrence of a theme (on the level of content) or of a
formula (on the level of form) in a given composition-in-performance refers
not only to its immediate context but also to all other analogous contexts remembered by the performer or by any member of the audience."[3] In other
words, Homeric references cannot be grasped from a purely synchronic point
of view. Similarly, I maintain that even the language of Homeric poetry, to
the extent that it continues the oral traditions from which it stems, "does not
and cannot belong to any one time, any one place: in a word, it *defies synchronic analysis.*"[4]

A synchronic perspective requires that Homeric poetry be viewed as a
system, not as a text. In order to analyze this system, however, a diachronic
perspective is also required.

Such an approach to Homeric poetry, combining as it does the diachronic
and synchronic perspectives, differs radically from approaches that adopt an
explicitly synchronic perspective.[5] One Homer critic, distancing himself
from those who explore "Indo-European and Near Eastern influences on the
poetry of archaic Greece," says of his own method: "I should note at this
point that I do not propose to treat the pre-Homeric history of many of the
ideas of this book; instead, I mean to give a *synchronic description* of their
significance within archaic Greek poetry."[6] Another critic makes this point
about his synchronic approach to Homeric poetry: "The analysis of system,
or the *synchronic approach,* is *logically prior to a diachronic approach* because systems are more intelligible than changes."[7]

Such a point applies admirably to the study of language per se: Saussure
himself advocated a synchronic perspective as a prerequisite for the diachronic.[8] But my counterpoint is that a purely synchronic perspective is in-

---

3. *PP* 50. See also above, Introduction, "Question 3."

4. *GM* 29, with reference to the extended discussion in Householder and Nagy 1972:19–23.

5. See Nagy 1999c:123–125. What I say there is restated here in this paragraph and in the two that follow it.

6. Ford 1992:16 n. 8. Emphasis mine. I note with interest that the diachronic dimension is described merely in terms of "influences," not derivations.

7. Peradotto 1990:13. Again, emphasis mine.

8. Saussure 1916:117: "Ainsi le linguiste qui veut comprendre cet état [that is, the system as per-

sufficient for reading Homer. The transmitted texts of the Homeric *Iliad* and *Odyssey* cannot be reduced to single speech-events, self-contained in one time and one place, as if we had direct access to actual recordings of the language of Homer.

Fieldwork in the study of oral poetry as it is performed requires a synchronic perspective, for purposes of describing the actual system perpetuated by the tradition. When it comes to delving into the principles of organization underlying the tradition, that is, the reality of cultural continuity, a diachronic perspective is also needed. Techniques of linguistic reconstruction can help explain otherwise opaque aspects of the language as it is current in the tradition: that is to say, the diachronic approach is needed to supplement the synchronic, as well as vice versa.[9]

There is a danger in restricting the field of vision to the synchronic. To say in Homeric criticism that the "world" or "worldview" that emerges from the structure of the *Iliad* and the *Odyssey* is the construct of one man at one time and place, or however many men from however many different times and places, risks the flattening out of the process of oral poetic creation, which requires analysis in the dimensions of both diachrony and synchrony.[10]

A purely synchronic approach to self-references in Homeric poetry, let alone references in general, leads to interpretations that can differ radically from those that rely on a combination of diachronic and synchronic perspectives. Moreover, the absence of a diachronic perspective can lead a synchronic observer to lose sight of any diachronic skewing altogether. In terms of my model of diachronic skewing, any synchronic reading of the skewed referent as if it were a simple statement of truth becomes in effect a misreading of the entire frame of reference. Such a misreading by a synchronic observer becomes a "synchronic skewing" of the evidence. Whereas diachronic skewing results from the tradition that is being studied, synchronic skewing is caused by the one who studies the tradition.[11]

We now come to a premier Homeric example of diachronic skewing, the image of the *aoidos* or 'singer' who sings as he accompanies himself on a

---

ceived through synchronic analysis] doit-il faire table rase de tout ce qui l'a produit et ignorer la diachronie." Cf. *PH* 4–5; also *GM* 35.

9. This paragraph is excerpted from *HQ* 17.

10. This paragraph is excerpted from *HQ* 20.

11. Most of my examples of "synchronic skewing" in the discussion that follows will be taken from Olson 1995.

stringed instrument called the *phorminx*. So goes the narrative of the *Odyssey* about the epic singing of Demodokos at a feast (8.67: *phorminx*; 8.73: *aoidos* 'singer' and *aeidemenai* 'sing').[12] The paradox here is that the medium of "Homer" has outgrown, as it were, the medium of Demodokos: it can be argued that the basic building block of Homeric poetry, the epic hexameter as we know it, had evolved out of a vast rhythmical repertoire of song-making traditions to become the distinctive poetic meter of a medium of performance characterized by (1) reduced melody and (2) absence of instrumental accompaniment.[13] Such characteristics of epic contradict the details about the medium of the epic performer as reported by epic.[14]

In the historical times of the Classical and Hellenistic periods, this medium of "Homer" was mediated by *rhapsōidoi* 'rhapsodes', professionals who performed at Panhellenic festivals and whose repertoire also included, besides the epic hexameters of Homer, poetry composed in two other metrical forms: elegiac distich and iambic trimeter.[15] For all intents and purposes, the professional medium of the rhapsode in the Classical period was restricted to these three nonmelodic (or at least "reduced melodic") meters of *poetry*; here we must contrast the fully melodic meters—or, more simply, the rhythms— of *song*, which was the professional medium of the citharode or lyre-singer (*kitharōidos*), as also of the aulode or reed-singer (*aulōidos*).[16] There is another paradox here, in that the Homeric visualization of the singer matches the Classical image of the citharode more closely than that of the rhapsode.[17]

---

12. Cf. *BA* 17–25.

13. The case is made at length in *PH* 17–24, where I trace the evolution of the epic hexameter into its nonmelodic (or at least reduced melodic) and nonaccompanied form. For an illuminating application of my discussion of the semantics of "singing" and "speaking," see Habinek 1998.

14. Besides my arguments in *PH* 17–24, see also Ford 1992:303, who likewise argues that the epic hexameter as we know it was nonmelodic and nonaccompanied. I think he goes too far, however, in implying that this form could switch back to a melodic and accompanied by-form. Such a by-form is the lyric hexameter, as attested in classical drama. But this lyric hexameter is not the same form as the epic hexameter, since it lacks the prosodic system of its epic counterpart. At p. 303 n. 24, Ford cites with approval West 1981, who assumes that Homeric references to Demodokos and Phemios provide a realistic picture of hexameter performance (for a critique of West's position, see *PH* 21).

15. *PH* 24–29.

16. *PH* 54, 85–87, 90, 98, 104, 107, 340–341. These pages include discussions of the interweavings of professional and amateur performance traditions.

17. *PH* 373. This formulation is the subtext for my choice of the image of a citharode as the cover for a book on Homeric questions (Nagy 1996b = *HQ*). I chose a rhapsode for *Homeric Responses*.

We see here the essence of what I call diachronic skewing: "Just as the Homeric testimony about the performance of epic by singers at feasts belies the synchronic reality of the performance of epic by rhapsodes at Panhellenic festivals, so also the Homeric testimony about the singer's singing to the accompaniment of the lyre belies the synchronic reality of the rhapsode's reciting without any accompaniment at all." [18]

Diachronic skewing works backward as well as forward in time: in other words, it can produce details that seem anachronistic from the viewpoint of earlier instead of later times. The Homeric visualization of the singer is retroactively affected by another synchronic reality that we may reconstruct for later stages in the historical period, that is, the principle of relay performance, where one competing rhapsode has to continue the epic narrative at the point where the previous competing rhapsode had "left off," as expressed by the verb *lēgō* 'leave off'; this verb is featured in two sources that refer explicitly to rhapsodic relays: Dieuchidas of Megara FGH 485 F 6, by way of Diogenes Laertius 1.57, and "Plato" *Hipparchus* 228b–c.

Anachronistically, the *Iliad* gives a stylized representation of such rhapsodic relay performance in the scene where Achilles is shown performing the epic songs of heroes, *klea andrōn* 'glories of men' at *Iliad* 9.189, while Patroklos is waiting for his own turn, in order to take up the song precisely where Achilles will have left off. Again, the verb is *lēgō* 'leave off':

τὸν δ' εὗρον φρένα τερπόμενον φόρμιγγι λιγείῃ
καλῇ δαιδαλέῃ, ἐπὶ δ' ἀργύρεον ζυγὸν ἦεν.
τὴν ἄρετ' ἐξ ἐνάρων πόλιν Ἠετίωνος ὀλέσσας·
τῇ ὅ γε θυμὸν ἔτερπεν, ἄειδε δ' ἄρα <u>κλέα ἀνδρῶν</u>.
Πάτροκλος δέ οἱ <u>οἶος</u> ἐναντίος ἧστο σιωπῇ,
<u>δέγμενος</u> Αἰακίδην <u>ὁπότε λήξειεν ἀείδων</u>.

And they [the members of the embassy] found him [Achilles] de-
  lighting his spirit with a clear-sounding lyre,
beautiful and well-wrought, and there was a silver bridge on it.
He won it out of the spoils after he destroyed the city of Eetion.

---

18. *PH* 24. A Homeric word like *aoidē* may be expected to mean 'song', and yet it applies to a form of performance that is distinctly not melodic song. See Ford 1992:305, who tries to resolve the problem by defining Homeric *aoidē* as 'unmelodic song'; but the point is, it *is* melodic song diachronically, reapplied to unmelodic song synchronically.

> Now he was delighting his spirit with it, and he sang the glories of
> men (*klea andrōn*).
> But *Patroklos*, all alone, was sitting, facing him, in silence,
> waiting for whatever moment the Aeacid would leave off (*lēgō*)
> singing.
>
> *Iliad* 9.186–191

I offer this interpretation:

> So long as Achilles alone sings the *klea andrōn* 'glories of men', these
> heroic glories cannot be heard by anyone but Patroklos alone. Once
> Achilles leaves off and Patroklos starts singing, however, the contin-
> uum that is the *klea andrōn*—the Homeric tradition itself—can at
> long last become activated. This is the moment awaited by *Patrokleēs*
> 'he who has the *klea* [glories] of the ancestors'. In this Homeric image
> of Patroklos waiting for his turn to sing, then, we have in capsule form
> the esthetics of rhapsodic sequencing.[19]

Using the term "evolution" in the broader sense of explicitly including
history as well as diachrony, I have already spoken of my "evolutionary
model" for the making of Homeric poetry.[20] A subset of this model, as we
have seen, is the argument for the evolution of the formal medium of this poetry, epic hexameter.[21]

Another subset of this model is the argument for the evolution of the me-
diators of this medium. In terms of my evolutionary model for the making
of Homeric poetry, the figure of the *rhapsōidos* 'rhapsode' is the very embodi-
ment of an evolving medium that continues, in the course of time, to put
more and more limitations on the process of recomposition-in-performance.
The succession of rhapsodes linking a Homer in the remote past with Ho-

---

19. *PP* 72–73. Cf. Ford 1992:115 n. 31, who notes the use of *lēgō* 'leave off' at the point in the
narrative where Demodokos leaves off his Trojan narrative (*Odyssey* 8.87); this verb, Ford argues, "is
the technical expression used by a rhapsode to end a performance or a part of one." For parallels,
he cites *Homeric Hymn to Dionysus* 17–18, Hesiod fr. 305.4 MW, and *Theogony* 48. He also cites
Dieuchidas of Megara FGH 485 F 6 (by way of Diogenes Laertius 1.57), already cited by me above,
and the line from the *Iliad* (9.191) that is presently under discussion. On this line, he refers to the
analysis by Dunkel 1979:268–269 (*lēgō* is "used of poetic competition").

20. See again above, Introduction, "Question 2."

21. I argued at length for this model already in *PH*, specifically invoking the term *evolve/evo-
lutionary* at pp. 11, 18, 21, 23–24, 53–54, 56–58, 82–84, 191, 196–198, 360, 415.

meric performances in the "present" of the historical period—as extrapolated from such accounts as Plato's *Ion*—is a *diachronic* reality. This reality can only be distorted by any attempt to arrive at a *synchronic* definition of rhapsodes, meant as some kind of foil for an idealized definition of Homer.[22]

This diachronic reality is also distorted, I shall now argue, by any attempt to force a *synchronic* definition of the singer's medium as represented by Homeric poetry. I choose as a case in point a book by Douglas Olson, who offers an exclusively synchronic point of view in interpreting the Homeric usage of the word *kleos*.[23] According to Olson's book, *kleos* in Homeric poetry means not 'glory' as conferred by poetry, which is the definition that I have developed from a combination of synchronic and diachronic points of view,[24] but simply 'oral report' about an event, object, or individual, and thus 'gossip' or 'news'.[25] The goal, for this book, is "to ask what *kleos* has to do with real life."[26] The problem is, the "real life" that is being imagined here as the empirical basis for the study of raw data is not real life but a poetic representation of real life.

"Real life" is conditioned by the medium of poetry that represents, however realistically, such "real life." I hold that the empirical basis has to be the tradition that produced the representation of "real life." On that basis, *within the medium of Homeric poetry*, *kleos* means the 'glory' that this medium confers upon events, objects, or individuals. Striking examples are *Iliad* 11.227 and 2.485–486.[27]

What may be "oral report" and even "gossip" or "news" in the short-range terms of "real life" as represented by epic narrative can still be the "glory" of epic in the long-range terms of what epic really does and is meant to do in its own historical context, which is, ultimately, to glorify its subject matter.[28]

---

22. This paragraph is excerpted from *HQ* 82. Cf. Dougherty 2001:29–30.

23. Olson 1995. An exclusively synchronic point of view is implicitly opposed to an evolutionary model for the making of Homeric poetry. At p. 25 n. 4, Olson describes himself as "believing that the *Odyssey* we have is a faithful copy of a song sung sometime in the late 8th century B.C.E."; I note with interest his emphasis on "faithful."

24. Nagy 1974:229–291, summarized in *BA* 16, 95.

25. Olson 1995:2: event (*Odyssey* 23.137–138; *Iliad* 11.21–22, 227–228, 13.364); object (*Iliad* 8.192–193); individual (*Odyssey* 3.83, 13.415); "gossip" or "news" (*Odyssey* 16.461; cf. 1.282–283; 2.216–217).

26. Olson 1995:2. For a critique of this kind of pseudo-empiricism, see *PH* 4.

27. As analyzed in *BA* 16–17.

28. For a comparable semantic phenomenon, where the overall concept of the medium subsumes individual contexts within it, see *PH* 218–219, on the usage of *apodeiknusthai* in the sense of 'perform' in Herodotus.

This historical context of epic is real life—and here I remove the quotation marks to stress the reality that eludes the perspective that I am criticizing.

From that perspective, instances of *kleos* in contexts like *Iliad* 11.227 and 2.485–486 must be ruled out as evidence for the overarching meaning of 'glory' *as conferred by the medium*. From that perspective, *Iliad* 11.227 must be merely a case of 'oral report';[29] as for 2.485–486, the *kleos* that is heard by the poet must be nothing more than "what is heard by individuals who were not present at an event," to be contrasted with "the knowledge of eye-witnesses (in this case the Muses)."[30] From that perspective, a Muse is nothing more than a poet's alternative way of referring to his own creativity in indulging his audience.[31]

Olson's book makes the overall claim that the singular of *kleos* "never obviously and unambiguously means specifically 'poetic glory' in either the *Odyssey* or the *Iliad*."[32] For supporting such a claim, it offers an appendix meant to refute my interpretation of *kleos aphthiton* 'imperishable glory' at *Iliad* 9.413.[33]

The argumentation of this appendix relies heavily on the earlier arguments of Margalit Finkelberg, against which I have already published a set of counterarguments.[34] There is therefore no need to rehearse here her points and my counterpoints. For the moment, I insist only on one thing: that Finkelberg has not succeeded, as Olson claims, in disproving my interpreta-

---

29. See again Olson 1995: 2; *Iliad* 11.227 is not even included in his index locorum.

30. Olson, ibid.: 13 n. 31.

31. I take special note of the scenario in Olson (ibid.: 14) where he seeks to derive song directly from the "real life" represented by Homeric song: "The culmination of this process of local gossip growing gradually into widespread, even universally known rumor and reputation is song." When song happens, according to this scenario, it comes out of the historical contingencies of rumors as portrayed in the "real life" of Homeric narrative: "If one of these stories becomes sufficiently popular in a place, one can assume, the local singer takes it up (esp. *Od.* 1.351–352; 8.73–75), relying on his Muse or, in less stylized or less mythologized terms, his own creative intelligence to supply the details for which men are so hungry."

32. Ibid.: 3 n. 2.

33. Ibid.: 224–227.

34. *PH* 244–245 n. 126, restated in *GM* 122–123 n. 3 and 127 n. 22. These discussions, and even the books in which they are to be found (with much more on *kleos*), are ignored in Olson 1995. (For criticisms of other omissions in this book, see Goldhill 1996.) For further arguments against Finkelberg's position, see Watkins 1995: 173–178. Although Watkins defends some aspects of my position, especially my arguments in Nagy 1974 based on an analysis of the poetics of Sappho, he does not cite my arguments against Finkelberg's position in *PH* and *GM*. Moreover, Watkins (p. 173) says that he does not fully agree with my position, either: "But since I differ from Nagy in certain crucial respects, and since his analysis apparently did not convince Finkelberg, I set forth briefly here

tion of *kleos aphthiton* as a noun-epithet combination.[35] Even if *aphthiton* in the context of the expression *kleos aphthiton estai* at 9.413 could be viewed synchronically as predicative rather than attributive (so that *kleos aphthiton estai* would match semantically the expression *kleos oupot' oleitai*, as at 2.325),[36] it would not follow that the attributive function can be ruled out from a diachronic point of view.[37] We need to reexamine in this regard the generative rules involving the syntax of attributive and predicative adjectives.[38]

---

my own apologia for *kleos aphthiton*." His discussion does not make the differences explicit. I address in notes 37 and 38 below what I think is one particular point of disagreement between his position and mine.

35. Olson 1995:226: "And that alone [that is, the claim that *kleos aphthiton* cannot be a noun-epithet combination] does fatal damage to Nagy's argument." But see now Volk 2002, esp. pp. 63, 66–67.

36. I continue to resist such a view, since the rhetoric of Achilles' statement at *Iliad* 9.413 has to do with the claim that he will have *kleos* in compensation for dying young, not that he already has a *kleos*. Achilles has to choose between dying young or dying old, and he has to make the first choice if he is to have *kleos* at all. He is not qualifying what kind of *kleos* he is to have: he is saying absolutely that he will possess *kleos,* and the absolute form of this possession is *kleos aphthiton*. See *BA*² xii–xiii. See also Nagy 1974:118–139, on *kleos aphthiton* in Sappho 44.4, where the epithet *aphthiton* must be attributive, not predicative. See now also Volk 2002, esp. p. 63.

37. As I scan the repertoire of epic expressions involving *kleos* plus variations on the verb "to be" as listed by Watkins 1995:174–175, I notice that he translates κλέος ἔσσεται ἐσθλόν (*kleos essetai esthlon*) at *Odyssey* 24.94 by making the adjective *esthlon* attributive, not predicative; by contrast, he translates κλέος ἄφθιτον ἔσται (*kleos aphthiton estai*) at *Iliad* 9.413 by making the adjective *aphthiton* predicative. The interpretation of *esthlon* as attributive at *Odyssey* 24.94 is understandable in terms of the many Homeric contexts where *esthlon* added to *kleos* must be taken in that sense (*Iliad* 5.3, 273; 17.16, 143; 22.514; *Odyssey* 1.95; 3.78, 380; 13.422). I note in particular a context that occurs in the immediate vicinity of κλέος ἄφθιτον ἔσται (*kleos aphthiton estai*) at *Iliad* 9.413, namely, ὤλετο μοι κλέος ἐσθλόν (*ōleto moi kleos esthlon*) at *Iliad* 9.415. Watkins (p. 175) concedes that *kleos . . . esthlon* at *Odyssey* 24.94 "can be translated predicatively," and then he goes on to say: "But it is in either case [that is, either in the attributive or in the predicative sense] only a transformation of the clearly formulaic κλέος ἐσθλόν (ἄροιτο) of *Il.* 5.3 et passim."

38. Following up on the argumentation of Watkins as discussed in the previous footnote, I must take my disagreement further. It needs to be pointed out that κλέος ἔσσεται ἐσθλόν (*kleos essetai esthlon*) at *Odyssey* 24.94 is just as "formulaic" as the κλέος ἐσθλὸν ἄροιτο (*kleos esthlon aroito*) of *Iliad* 5.3. Also, the term "transformation" can mislead if it is taken to mean here that one phrase is derived from another. From a synchronic point of view, both phrases *kleos essetai esthlon* and *kleos esthlon aroito* are generated by the same formulaic system. From a diachronic point of view, on the other hand, the combination *kleos esthlon* derives, of and by itself, from a combination of noun plus attributive adjective, as still attested in various syntactical patterns of Homeric diction where *esthlon* must be attributive from a synchronic point of view, as in the accusative construction of κλέος ἐσθλὸν ἄροιτο (*kleos esthlon aroito*) at *Iliad* 5.3. We may still leave open the possibility that the combination of *kleos* plus verb "to be" plus *esthlon* derives, of and by itself, from a combination of noun plus predicative adjective. But we cannot assume that the predicative usage derives from the attributive usage. Conversely, we cannot assume that the attributive usage of *kleos aphthiton* derives from the predicative usage that is claimed by Finkelberg and others for *kleos aphthiton estai* at *Iliad* 9.413. Such an assumption would not make sense from a diachronic point of view.

It has been claimed that "the Vedic phrase on which Nagy founds his thesis is a hypothetical form reconstructed on the basis of *Rig-Veda* 1.40.4; 8.103.5; 9.66.7; and 1.9.7bc (where the two words appear in different lines), so that the argument is speculative from the very first."[39] This claim serves as basis for a further claim: "No evidence of any other sort has ever been put forward in favor of the thesis, beyond some vague alleged parallels in the *Rig-Veda*, which of and by themselves prove nothing."[40] The major problem with this critique of my argumentation is that it lacks diachronic perspective. My painstaking diachronic analysis of the Vedic forms has been either ignored or overlooked.[41] We see here, I submit, an extreme case of "synchronic skewing."

I conclude by taking one last look at the concept of diachronic skewing. The word "skewing," as I noted at the beginning, implies a slanted perspective, as if by way of squinting. The vision is distorted, with one side or direction unduly emphasized over another. The distortion, however, seems to be coming from the tradition itself, not from the vision of the empirical observer of that tradition. Still, the viewer may have to squint in order to see the patterns of overemphasis and underemphasis. A judicious combination of synchronic and diachronic perspectives is needed to balance the vision.

---

39. Olson 1995:227 n. 11. The "hypothetical form" to which he refers is *śravas* and its epithet *akṣitam*. There is nothing hypothetical about either of these Vedic words, nor about the combination of these words as a single noun + epithet expression in *Rig-Veda* 1.9.7bc. The fact that the noun and its epithet are separated from each other by intervening phraseology in *Rig-Veda* 1.9.7bc (technically, "tmesis" of noun + epithet) does not render the actual combination *śravas* + *akṣitam* "hypothetical." In Nagy 1974:191–228, I demonstrate that the metrical line-placements of this noun and its epithet are predictable in terms of traditional Vedic phraseology and meter. There exists an overall Vedic system of alternating tmesis/contiguity in noun + epithet combinations (see esp. Nagy 1974:210). As I also demonstrate, there is a cognate system of noun + epithet combinations in archaic Greek poetics. Since I cannot agree with Olson's version of my "thesis," I should assert here my own version, in its simplest form: the combination of *śravas* and its epithet *akṣitam* in Vedic poetry is cognate—both metrically and phraseologically—with the combination of *kleos* and its epithet *aphthiton* in Greek poetry. If indeed the combinations are cognate, then the poetic systems that generated these combinations are also cognate. See now also Volk 2002.

40. Olson 1995:227; Olson is arguing here with Edwards 1988:30.

41. I value the words of Watkins 1995:173 on my combining of synchronic and diachronic perspectives: "Gregory Nagy in numerous publications [1974, 1979, 1990b] has rightly focused on the importance of distinguishing the synchronic and the diachronic in the study of formulas." In general response to Olson's arguments, I stress Watkins's next sentence: "The diachronic may be within a single tradition, without recourse to comparison." In Nagy 1974:191–228, my reconstruction of the unattested Vedic combination *śravas* + *akṣitam* (in contiguity, versus the attested combination in tmesis) as a cognate of Greek *kleos* + *aphthiton* was based on a diachronic analysis of the Vedic phraseology and metrics—an analysis that was independent of the additional comparison with the Greek.

 Chapter 3

Irreversible Mistakes and Homeric Clairvoyance

In "oral poetry," mistakes can and do happen in the process of composition-in-performance. Such mistakes, including major mistakes in narration, are documented in the fieldwork of Milman Parry and Albert Lord on South Slavic oral poetic traditions.[1] For a striking example, we may turn to Lord's account, in *The Singer of Tales,* of a singer who made the same mistake in plot construction when he sang the "same" song in a performance recorded seventeen years after an earlier recording.[2] In an article entitled "The Homeric Poems as Oral Dictated Texts," Richard Janko claims to have found such mistakes in the *Iliad* and the *Odyssey,* summing up his views this way: "Poets composing orally cannot go back and alter what they have composed."[3] With due allowance for differences in contexts, he compares the words of Horace *Ars Poetica* 390: *nescit vox missa reverti.* I find it noteworthy that Janko speaks of poets who cannot "alter what they have composed," not of poets who cannot "alter what they have performed." His idea, then, is that Homeric composition is irreversible and that therefore any mistakes in Homeric composition are likewise irreversible. In what follows, I take issue with such an idea. I propose to reconsider the two central Homeric examples chosen by Janko, and I suggest alternative ways of interpreting what he thinks are irreversible mistakes.

The two examples of Homeric "mistakes" are (1) references to the weather in *Odyssey* 20.103–106 and 113–114, and (2) the use of duals instead of plurals in the "Embassy Scene" of *Iliad* 9, about which we are told: "But Homer

---

The original version of this chapter is Nagy 1999b.

1. The central works, again, are [M.] Parry *MHV* and Lord 1960, 1991, 1995.
2. Lord 1960:28.
3. Janko 1998b:7.

never went back to erase the tell-tale duals."[4] Janko's interpretation of such "mistakes" depends on his "dictation theory." I disagree with this theory. On the other hand, for reasons I have already explained, I have no reason to disagree with the "dictation theory" of Albert Lord.[5] Moreover, I should stress that Lord's general idea of Homeric oral composition-in-performance, which is foundational for my argument, is not at all dependent on his "dictation theory."[6]

This chapter is divided into two parts. In the first, I argue generally, in purely poetic terms, that the two Homeric examples chosen by Janko involve not "mistakes" but just the opposite, feats of artistic virtuosity. In the second part, I go on to argue more specifically that such virtuosity can be appreciated in *oral* poetic terms.

Let us begin with the extended passage known as the "Embassy Scene" in *Iliad* 9, featuring dual forms where we may have expected the plural. In Homeric scholarship during the last half century or so, the ongoing debate centers on this question about the embassy sent to Achilles and comprised of Phoenix, Ajax, Odysseus, and the two heralds Odios and Eurybates: Do the dual forms in this passage refer to Ajax and Odysseus, excluding Phoenix, or can they refer to Phoenix and Ajax, potentially excluding Odysseus?[7]

Already in the Hellenistic era, scholars who produced editions and commentaries of Homer disagreed about these tell-tale duals, and their disagreements reflect the inherent problems as they persist to this day. According to Aristarchus (middle of the second century B.C.E.), the usage of dual forms to express plural meanings was ungrammatical for Homer; according to Zenodotus (early third century) and Crates (middle of the second century and earlier), such a usage was grammatical.[8]

For Aristarchus, the duals in the Embassy Scene had to be explained as referring only to two persons rather than three, and his solution was to argue

---

4. Ibid.: 8.

5. Again, Lord 1953, later reprinted in Lord 1991:3–48, with an addendum.

6. As Casey Dué pointed out to me, Lord in the 1991 addendum (pp. 47–48; repeated for emphasis at pp. 11–12) raises important questions centering on the idea that composition-in-dictation may be different artistically—or even cognitively—from oral composition-in-performance without dictation.

7. The most informative and insightful summary of the ongoing debate, I find, is Wilson 2002:71–108.

8. See Broggiato 1998.

that Phoenix is not really one of the ambassadors. According to this explanation, the only ambassadors are Odysseus and Ajax.

The essential verses are 9.169–170: Nestor says that Phoenix ἡγησάσθω 'should lead' the embassy (169) and ἔπειτα 'then' Ajax and Odysseus should follow along (170). Aristarchus thought that only the second two of these three persons were ambassadors, arguing that ἔπειτα indicates *posteriority* on the level of action (ἔπειτα = μετὰ ταῦτα, Scholia A to *Iliad* 9.169a). By contrast, Crates thought that ἔπειτα here indicates *simultaneity* on the level of action and posteriority only on the level of narration (Scholia A, ibid.; ἔπειτα = δή, as also in the case of ἔπειτα at *Iliad* 13.586).[9] Here as elsewhere, it appears that Aristarchus was arguing against Crates rather than the other way around, and that Crates represented the received opinion of earlier generations of scholars.[10]

There are other details, besides the point made by Crates about ἔπειτα 'then' at *Iliad* 9.170, that need to be brought to bear as well. For example, whereas Nestor says that Phoenix ἡγησάσθω 'should lead' the embassy (9.169), and ἔπειτα 'then' Ajax and Odysseus should follow along (9.170), we see at a later point in the narrative that it is Odysseus who now leads the embassy as the ensemble approaches the tent of Achilles:

τὼ δὲ βάτην προτέρω, <u>ἡγεῖτο δὲ δῖος Ὀδυσσεύς</u>

The two of them went ahead, and radiant Odysseus <u>was leading</u>.

Iliad 9.192

Nestor had said at 9.169 that Phoenix should lead, but now we see at 9.192 that Odysseus is leading. What has happened in the interim? Why is Odysseus now leading instead of Phoenix, and who are the two characters that must now be following? How can Ajax and Odysseus be the followers, now that Odysseus is leading?

Let us take a second look at "the two of them" at this point in the narrative, 9.192.[11] At the earliest point in the narrative, 9.170, "the two of them"

---

9. See Scholia A to *Iliad* 13.586a and the commentary of Broggiato 1998:140 n. 15.

10. On scholiastic evidence for situations where Aristarchus reacts to Crates' editorial and exegetical judgments about the Homeric text, see Broggiato 1998:141; also Nagy 1998a:219–223.

11. *HQ* 141 n. 123, with bibliography. Two possibilities are considered there: Does the dual refer here to Ajax and Odysseus, so that Odysseus as leader is included in the dual, or (as I prefer)

must be Ajax and Odysseus, as I have just noted. Then, at 9.182, the "two of them" would still appear to be Ajax and Odysseus by default.[12]

For Zenodotus and Crates, we may infer, the dual in both 9.182 and 9.192 does not even have to refer specifically to two persons only. In fact, the edition of Homer by Zenodotus accepted textual variants that featured dual forms in contexts where the sense clearly requires plural entities.[13] Such patterns of editorial as well as poetic justification help explain the explicit usage of dual-for-plural in the poetics of the Hellenistic era.[14]

Thus when Achilles finally greets the ambassadors by using dual forms at *Iliad* 9.197–198, after having gestured to "the two of them," in the dual (again), at 9.196, I infer that the likes of Zenodotus and Crates interpreted the references simply as dual-for-plural usage. Although we may find "no *grammatical* justification," in terms of archaic Greek poetic diction, for the use of the dual in place of plural,[15] there may be a *poetic* justification. To the extent that the poetry has its own grammar, we may still say that Achilles is "grammatically correct."[16]

What seems to be at work in the Embassy Scene and elsewhere is a poetics of *cross-reference* between older and newer versions.[17] My overall argument is that we see here the leaving-in of older elements and their recombination

---

does it refer to Phoenix and Ajax, so that Odysseus as leader is excluded from the dual? Louden (2002:75) argues that the dual refers to Phoenix and the herald Eurybates, so that Odysseus as leader is excluded, again, from the dual. I find this explanation unconvincing. In his article, Louden attempts to reconstruct an "underlying type scene" (p. 63) in order to account for most, if not all, of the variations he finds in the embassy scenes of the *Iliad* and in related passages. I see serious problems with Louden's assumption of a "basic" (p. 64) or "original" (p. 76) version. Also, when he says that a verse like *Iliad* 9.192 serves as an "archetype" for other verses (p. 72), I can accept his formulation only to the extent that the ambiguity of referents in such a verse may lead to further opportunities for variation. For example, the leader may or may not be included in the reference made by the dual construction (see the previous discussion). I agree, in any case, with Louden's point that the Odysseus figure was associated with dual constructions in his own right. Also, I value Louden's observations about the thematic affinity of Odysseus with the herald Eurybates.

    12. See *HQ* 139–140, esp. with reference to *Iliad* 1.387 as parallel to 9.182. This discussion is ignored by Louden (2002:74 n. 18).

    13. See the scholia to *Iliad* 1.567, 3.459, 6.112, 8.503, 13.627, 15.347, 18.287, 23.753; *Odyssey* 1.38, 8.251; cf. Rengakos 1993:76 n. 4; also Broggiato 1998:138 n. 5.

    14. See the analysis of Rengakos 1993:76–78.

    15. *BA* 49 par. 9 n. 1.

    16. *BA* 56 par. 20 n. 6.

    17. *BA*² xvii. I emphasize here the relative distinction between older and newer forms, as opposed to an absolutizing distinction between "original" and "derivative." For more on "cross-referencing" in terms of oral poetics, see the introduction above, "Question 4."

with newer elements, resulting in newer effects. The retention of the older dual forms can serve the special purpose of expressing "an archaic situation where there *should* be only two ambassadors even though there are now three."[18] There may be an interesting side-effect resulting from such a retention of the dual constructions: Achilles, in addressing two instead of three ambassadors (*Iliad* 9.197), thereby potentially snubs one of the three, Odysseus, in the context of a newer situation re-created out of an older one.[19] In this newer situation, the potential "exclusion" of Odysseus by Achilles' use of the dual becomes what may be called an artistic "masterstroke."[20]

The artistry of recombining older and newer narrative elements in the Embassy Scene is marked by the ostentatious usage of words referring to visual signals involving exchanges of looks between characters in the narrative, as if to signal communication that is not stated explicitly by way of words. At *Iliad* 9.196, for example, Achilles acknowledges eye contact with the ambassadors by pointing toward them (δεικνύμενος) as they approach him—and the pronoun form for 'them' is in the dual (τώ). At *Iliad* 9.167, Nestor says that the ambassadors to be chosen by him will be the ones that he looks at: ἐπιόψομαι 'I will look [in their direction]'. Presumably, he will exchange looks with each one in turn. Only in the verses that follow, 9.168–170, does he actually name his three choices. Needless to say, the looking and the naming can be imagined as simultaneous. Still, the point is that Nestor makes his expectation explicit already at 9.167: the chosen ones are to agree to be ambassadors at the very moment that he looks at them—and the verb form for 'let them agree' is in the dual (πιθέσθων). Later, at *Iliad* 9.180, Nestor is described as δενδίλλων 'blinking, making eyes' in the direction of 'each' of the ambassadors (ἐς ἕκαστον), 'especially at Odysseus' ('Οδυσσῆϊ δὲ μάλιστα), just as they are about to set off on their embassy.

The most striking example of visual signals involving exchanges of looks is yet to come in the Embassy Scene. It involves the use of *noeō* 'take note' in response to *neuō* 'nod' at *Iliad* 9.223. When the time comes for the speech-making to start in the Embassy Scene, Ajax makes the gesture of nodding (*neuō*) to Phoenix (9.223), whom we may have expected to be the first speaker, but it is Odysseus who takes note (*noeō*) of the gesture (223), fills a cup with

---

18. Nagy 1997c:179–180, with reference to *HQ* 138–145 and to *BA* 42–58.
19. Ibid.
20. *BA* 54.

wine, gestures (δείδεκτ') to Achilles (224), and begins to speak, thus becoming the first of the three speakers to address Achilles (225–306). As I have argued elsewhere, Odysseus is behaving like a "trickster" here: he is violating heroic etiquette by (1) acting like a host in a situation where he is a guest, and (2) speaking out of turn, contrary to the prearranged plan.[21]

The wording that describes the intervention of Odysseus is suggestive:

νεῦσ' Αἴας Φοίνικι· νόησε δὲ δῖος 'Οδυσσεύς.

Ajax nodded (neuō) to Phoenix. But radiant Odysseus took note (noeō).

Iliad 9.223

The verb *noeō* 'take note, notice, perceive', as I have argued elsewhere, is a special word used in archaic Greek poetic diction in contexts where a special interpretation, a special "reading," as it were, is signaled.[22] In passages like *Odyssey* 17.281[23] and *Iliad* 23.305,[24] it is clear that the verb *noeō* designates a complex level of understanding that entails two levels of meaning, one of which is overt while the other, the more important one, is latent. When Odysseus 'took note', νόησε (*noeō*), at *Iliad* 9.223, he was in effect taking an initiative with an ulterior motive, a latent purpose, in mind. As Cedric Whitman argues, the offer to Achilles by Agamemnon, as reformulated by Odysseus in his quoted speech from the Embassy Scene, endangers the very status of Achilles in epic.[25] It may be argued further that a potential ulterior motive of Odysseus, to undermine the heroic stature of Achilles, is understood by Achilles.[26] We recall what Achilles says: whoever says one thing and hides

---

21. *HQ* 142. For another situation where Odysseus speaks out of turn, see Muellner 1976:21 on *Odyssey* 14.439; corroboration by Wilson 2002:83 and 200 n. 41. See also *BA* 40 par. 17 n. 2 on *Odyssey* 8.474–483, where Odysseus is the guest of Alkinoos but acts like the host of Demodokos in offering the singer a choice cut of meat.

22. *GM* 202–222.

23. *GM* 208.

24. *GM* 217–219.

25. Whitman 1958:191–192. Cf. Martin 1989:116–117, 123. See now also Wilson 2002:85, which demonstrates how "Odysseus seems to have repaired Agamemnon's culturally objectionable offer." As Wilson points out (ibid.), "Odysseus omits any reference to compensation. His speech contains no compensation theme, no recognition of the harm Agamemnon had inflicted, and no resolution to Achilleus' *poinē* [revenge] theme."

26. *BA* 52–53. When I say "understood by Achilles," of course I mean it only in the sense that the understanding conveyed by the overall narrative is in such cases subjectively transferred, by the narrator, to the hero of the narrative. Cf. Martin 1989:197 n. 82, 210–212.

something else in his thoughts is as *ekhthros* 'hateful' to him as the gates of Hades (9.312–313). By implication, Achilles is portrayed as understanding a latent strategy of deceit on the part of Odysseus.[27] It may be that such a subtle understanding on the part of Achilles justifies the formalistic use of the dual in Achilles' greeting of the emissaries: this greeting in effect snubs Odysseus by excluding him from the ranks of those who are *philoi*, near and dear, to Achilles.[28]

To sum up my analysis of the Embassy Scene, I hold that the "formalistic" use of dual forms amounts to a virtuoso redeployment of two levels of meaning, one of which is overt while the other, the more important one, is latent.

We now come to the second of Janko's two prime examples of "irreversible mistakes" in Homer. As in the case of the Embassy Scene, I will first argue more generally, in purely poetic terms, that this second example chosen by Janko involves not a "mistake" but just the opposite, a feat of artistic virtuosity. Then and only then, as I have already indicated, will I go on to argue more specifically that the virtuosity can be appreciated in *oral* poetic terms.

The second example in question comes from the *Odyssey*. We see Odysseus in the act of praying to Zeus for *both* an omen *and* a *phēmē* 'prophetic utterance' as indications that he will indeed prevail over the suitors (20.98–101). Zeus responds by sending *both* thunder (20.103–104) *and* a *phēmē* (20.105).

The *phēmē* takes the form of a prayer uttered by an anonymous woman grinding grain with her mill (20.112–119): she is not sure for whom the sign of the god's thunder is intended (τεῳ, 20.114), but she prays to Zeus that he should intend it for her, too (καὶ ἐμοί, 20.115), by bringing to fulfillment the *epos* 'utterance' that she now speaks (20.115). The narrative framing her utterance likewise refers to the woman's prayer as an *epos*, adding that this *epos* is meant to be a *sēma* 'sign' for Odysseus (20.111).

As I have argued elsewhere, the poetic format of what the woman is "quoted" as saying is evident from such "milling songs" as *Carmina popularia*

---

27. *BA* 52–53. See also Wilson 2002:85, "Achilleus' acid response unmasks the trickster's deception, revealing that he is not taken in by Odysseus' rhetoric." As Wilson argues (ibid.), an essential aspect of this rhetoric is the moment when Odysseus replaces Agamemnon's objectionable term *apereisi' apoina* 'unlimited ransom' (*Iliad* 9.120) with his own neutralized term *axia dōra* 'worthy gifts' (*Iliad* 9.261).

28. This paragraph is an expanded version of *HQ* 142–143.

[*PMG*] no. 869.[29] It is also evident from the use of *epos,* which is attested in archaic poetic diction as meaning not just 'utterance' but also specifically 'poetic utterance'.[30]

For Janko, an irreversible mistake can be found here in what seems to be a contradiction between the words of the narrative framing the *phēmē* and the words of the "quoted" *phēmē* itself. In the words of the *phēmē* uttered by the woman, she says that the thundering of Zeus came from the starry sky (οὐρανοῦ ἀστερόεντος, 20.113), where no cloud is to be seen: οὐδέ ποθι νέφος ἐστί 'and there is not a cloud (*nephos*) anywhere' (20.114). This, then, was the sign that the woman had received: it was a thundering from a clear sky. By contrast, the narrative that frames her utterance refers to the thundering of Zeus, from radiant Olympus (ἀπ' αἰγλήεντος Ὀλύμπου, 20.103), and the thundering had come ὑψόθεν ἐκ νεφέων 'from on high, from out of the clouds (*nephea*)' (20.104).

Of course, no Homer critic would have any problem if the narrative frame here had been simpler, featuring only one sign—that is, if Odysseus had prayed for only one sign, the thunder of Zeus. The problem seems to arise from the combining of two signs in the narration—the thunder of Zeus and the song of the woman. It is this combination that has led to what appears to be a contradiction between these two signs. And yet, I propose that the combining of two narrative signs here amounts to an artistic narratological elaboration, which succeeds in producing a special poetic effect by way of juxtaposing the perceptions of the woman and the perceptions of Odysseus.

For the woman, only one sign had been needed, the thundering of Zeus, and that is the sign that she received. For Odysseus, however, the thundering of Zeus was not the complete sign that he had prayed for. It was an incomplete sign. In terms of his own prayer, it had to be completed, complemented, by a prophetic utterance, which turned out to be the *phēmē* of the woman. That utterance, however, could not become a completed *phēmē* for Odysseus unless Zeus heeded it on its own terms, on the woman's terms. For the woman, the thundering of Zeus came from a clear sky. For Odysseus, the same thun-

---

29. *GM* 221. The quotation is by way of Plutarch *Banquet of the Seven Sages* 157e (note esp. the wording that introduces the "quotation" of the singing woman in Eresos, τῆς ξένης ἤκουον ᾀδούσης πρὸς τὴν μύλην).

30. Again, *GM* 221.

dering had come from a clouded sky, and the message of Zeus became clear only after the woman received her own message from a clear sky. The utterance of the woman, an incipient *epos* that was as yet unclear for her, became a finished *epos* that was indeed clear for Odysseus, just as the thundering of Zeus shifted perceptually from a clouded to a clear sky. For Odysseus, the clarification and hence the fulfillment of the *epos* of the woman makes this *epos* into a genuine prophetic utterance—a *phēmē* (20.100, 105) or *kleēdōn* (20.120). The woman's speech has now become fulfilled as a speech-act. Her speech—or song—has now become an act of special prophecy, of cledonomancy.[31]

The prophecy, of course, starts with Zeus, whose thundering is in itself the primal act that leads to the cledonomancy. Zeus himself is ultimately prophetic in his manifestations of weather, and his meaning can be ambivalently bright or dark, clear or cloudy, positive or negative. The Indo-European form **dyeu-*, which becomes Greek *Zeus* (Ζεύς), means basically 'sky', thus conveying a cledonomantic ambivalence: it portends either clear or clouded weather. Despite this ambivalence of clear or clouded, positive or negative, in the meaning 'sky', the Indo-European noun **dyeu-* stems from the verb **diw-*, which has only the positive meaning 'be bright/clear', not the negative 'be dark/cloudy'—which is the other side of Zeus.

There is a similar cledonomantic ambivalence in the meaning of the Indo-European form **nebhos*, which becomes Greek *nephos* (νέφος) 'cloud': it means basically 'cloud' in ambivalently good or bad weather. This ambivalence explains the fact that in some Indo-European languages the derivative of **nebhos* means primarily 'sky', by way of metonymy. Such is the case with Russian *nebo* 'sky'. Thus in Russian idiom, *na nebe ni oblaka* means 'there's not a cloud (*oblako*) in the sky (*nebo*)'. From the standpoint of Indo-European linguistics, we see here a new word for 'cloud', *oblako*, while the old word for 'cloud' has become, metonymically, the new word for 'sky'. This new word can even stand for a cloudless sky, as in the idiom we have just seen: *na nebe ni oblaka* means 'there's not a cloud (*oblako*) in the sky (*nebo*)'.

Such a metonymic sense of Indo-European **nebhos* as 'sky' is visible also in some Homeric usages of the noun *nephos/nephea* 'cloud'/'clouds', which is

---

31. At the moment of fulfillment, Odysseus rejoices at both omens: (1) the prophetic utterance, *kleēdōn*, and (2) the thundering of Zeus (χαῖρεν δὲ κλεηδόνι . . . | Ζηνός τε βροντῇ, *Odyssey* 20.120–121).

potentially ambivalent in its own right concerning questions of good or bad weather. When Zeus thunders ὑψόθεν ἐκ νεφέων 'from on high, from out of the clouds (*nephea*)' in *Odyssey* 20.105, he is thundering from the sky, through the metonymy of the clouds. In this case, the ambivalence of clouds or sky is canceled only by the explicit statement, in the words of the singing woman at 20.114, that there is no *nephos* 'cloud' in the sky. In all other Homeric attestations, the potential metonymic sense of *nephos/nephea* as 'sky' can remain in force. A particularly striking example of this metonymic sense of 'sky' is evident at *Iliad* 13.523–524, where Zeus is pictured as sitting in grand isolation on the summit of Olympus, under a shining canopy of 'golden *nephea*' (ἀλλ' ὁ γὰρ ἄκρῳ Ὀλύμπῳ ὑπὸ χρυσέοισι νέφεσσιν | ἧστο).[32] At that moment in the narrative, the god is described as 'wrapped up' in his own thoughts, which are conventionally called the Will of Zeus (Διὸς βουλῆσιν ἐελμένος, 13.524).

I propose, in fact, that the theme of the Will of Zeus, as a conventional plot device of Homeric narrative, is essential for understanding the double omen of Zeus's thunder and the woman's song in the *Odyssey*. I propose, further, that the weather in this passage of the *Odyssey* depends on the Will of Zeus, and that the sudden shift from a cloudy to a clear sky is a choice in Homeric narratology, not a mistake in Homeric meteorology.

Moreover, the sudden shift from cloudy to clear skies can happen only after the narrative makes it clear that there is not a cloud in the sky. Before that clarification, it was left unclear whether or not the sky was cloudy. If the thundering of Zeus comes out of a clear blue (or, in this case, 'starry') sky, it is a bigger omen than if it comes out of a cloudy sky. If Odysseus had prayed for just one omen, not two, it would not be clear whether the thundering of Zeus had happened in cloudy or in clear weather. Since he prayed for two omens, however, and since the second omen was granted, now everything is clear, and the prophecy is augmented.[33]

---

32. Scholia V to *Odyssey* 20.104 actually cite this Iliadic passage, explaining the usage of *nephea* at 20.104 in terms of metonymy. A similar explanation is offered in Scholia BQ: that the word *nephea* at *Odyssey* 20.104 is to be understood as referring to a realm where clouds can be expected to happen.

33. Cf. the analysis of this double omen in Austin 1975:119–121. With reference to *Odyssey* 20.92–101, Austin remarks (ibid.: 119): "Just before [Odysseus] falls asleep on the eve of his vengeance, outside his palace, Athena appears at his head to give him encouragement; just before the following dawn he hears Penelope's lament . . . and imagines that she has recognized him and is standing at his head. Athena and Penelope appear like two dream figures but with contrary import.

The shift from a clouded sky to a clear one depends on the clarification of the Will of Zeus in the course of the narrative. Further, the *sēma* 'sign' meant by Zeus for Odysseus (20.111) depends implicitly on the faculty for both encoding and decoding it, and that faculty is conventionally expressed by the noun *noos* and the verb *noeō*.[34] This same word *noeō*, as we have just seen, designates the faculty for decoding the ulterior meanings of the Embassy Scene.

The *noos* or 'intentionality' of Zeus is key to understanding the plot-constructions of Homeric narrative. In the *Iliad*, for example, when Zeus expresses his Will by nodding his head (1.524–527), Hera reacts by chiding him for not telling what it is that he really intends—literally, for not making an *epos* out of what he has in his *noos* (*noeō*, 1.543). Zeus replies that the *muthos* 'utterance' he has in his *noos* (*noeō*, 1.549) is for him alone to know. And yet, the Homeric audience may already know, since the *Iliad* declares programmatically that its plot *is* the Will of Zeus (1.5).[35]

To sum up, I repeat my earlier formulation: when Zeus thunders ὑψόθεν ἐκ νεφέων 'from on high, from out of the clouds (*nephea*)' (*Odyssey* 20.105), he is essentially thundering from the sky, through the metonymy of the clouds. This poetic description in the framing narrative does not contradict, per se, the later perception of a clear sky within the framed speech: οὐδέ ποθι νέφος ἐστί 'and there is not a cloud (*nephos*) anywhere' (20.114). But that later perception does indeed clarify the earlier narrative perception of a sky that *may* be clouded over. Now the sky is clear, as the cledonomantic words have finally been clarified.

The time has come to rethink the two Homeric passages that we have examined, one from the *Iliad* and the other from the *Odyssey*, in terms of oral poetics, not just poetics per se. I hold that the complexities of these passages reflect the accretions of a highly sophisticated oral poetic tradition that kept on recombining its older and its newer elements in the productive phases of its evolution. These older and newer elements may at times seem to contradict each other if we stop and view each of them as individual parts, but I suggest that such contradictions were transcended by the actual recombinations

---

Penelope weeping seems to be a bad omen which annuls Athena as good omen. It is a further complication that *the good omen happens at night, the bad one just at dawn* [emphasis mine]." As Austin argues (p. 120), Odysseus's prayer for a double omen is meant as a resolution to the Athena-Penelope omens.

34. *GM* 221, with reference to *sēma* 'sign' in this passage of the *Odyssey*, 20.111.
35. *GM* 222.

of these parts into the totality of an ongoing system that we know as Homeric poetry. In order to account for such an ongoing system, I developed my evolutionary model for the making of Homeric poetry, and it is this model that I seek to test in what follows.

This testing of my theory will require a confrontation with two alternative theories: (1) Homeric literacy, and (2) Homeric dictation. The first of these theories, as formulated by Adam Parry and others, requires a Homer who is too sophisticated for oral poetry. The second, as formulated by Janko, allows for a Homer who is capable of making major as well as minor mistakes in composition and who is therefore lacking in the kind of sophistication that typifies the written poetry of later periods. Both of these formulations, I submit, undervalue the potential of artistic sophistication in oral poetry. My evolutionary model, by contrast, is designed to explore that potential to the fullest.

Let me begin the testing of my model by affirming the obvious: I have no doubts that irreversible mistakes could indeed have happened at any given moment of performance in the Homeric tradition. But the fundamental question is, Did such mistakes persist in the transmission of the Homeric text? This question is linked to another one, which is even more fundamental: To what extent can we apply to the text of Homer the empirical findings of Parry and Lord concerning composition-in-performance in the South Slavic oral traditions?

I stress *empirical findings* about oral poetics because there are those who speak of the "Parry-Lord theory" as if oral poetry were just that, a theory, rather than an observable fact, established by the empirical study of living oral traditions. And I ask my question because I recognize the distinction between theory and fact whenever we apply such empirical findings to the Homeric text:

> The existence of oral poetry is a fact, ascertained by way of fieldwork. The application of what we know inductively about oral poetry to the text of the *Iliad* and the *Odyssey*, or to any other text, is not an attempt to prove a "theory" about oral poetry. If we are going to use the word *theory* at all in such a context, it would be more reasonable to say that Parry and Lord had various *theories* about the affinity of Homeric poetry with what we know as oral poetry.[36]

---

36. *HQ* 20. My formulation here, as quoted from *HQ*, is echoed by Janko 1998b:4.

In order to see what exactly is at stake whenever we compare a living oral tradition, South Slavic or otherwise, with what we find in the Homeric text as we have it, it is essential to review briefly the comparative methodology shared by Parry and Lord.

The methods of Parry and Lord are linked with the basics of the academic discipline that we know today as Comparative Literature.[37] Even more fundamentally, they are linked with the *méthode comparative* of historical linguistics, especially as exemplified by Antoine Meillet.[38] In the collected writings of Milman Parry, published in 1971 by his son, Adam Parry, under the title *The Making of Homeric Verse,* we can see explicit references to the decisive influence of Meillet. The most dramatic such reference by Milman Parry can be found in his "Ćor Huso: A Study of Southslavic Song," an unfinished work dating from his final years, 1933 to 1935.[39] In his preliminary notes for the planned foreword to that work, Milman Parry explicitly recognizes the importance of the living South Slavic oral traditions as a central comparandum for the study of Homer, and he attributes to Meillet the impetus for this recognition:

> My first studies were on the style of the Homeric poems and led me to understand that so highly formulaic a style could be only traditional. I failed, however, at the time to understand as fully as I should have that a style such as that of Homer must not only be traditional but also must be oral. It was largely due to the remarks of my teacher M. Antoine Meillet that I came to see, dimly at first, that a true understanding of the Homeric poems could only come with a full understanding of the nature of oral poetry.[40]

It is a curious twist in the history of the study of oral poetics that Milman Parry's debt to Meillet, which he clearly recognizes here and elsewhere,[41] is

---

37. On this discipline, see Guillén 1993, esp. pp. 173–179, with reference to Parry and Lord; also Davidson 2000:xiii–xiv. Lord, during his years as professor at Harvard University, was an active member of the Comparative Literature Department. His book, *The Singer of Tales,* was originally published as volume 24 (1960) of that department's monograph series, Harvard Studies in Comparative Literature.

38. A fundamental work on the comparative method is Meillet 1925; cf. Nagy 1974:19–20.

39. Fragments of this work have been published in *MHV* [1933–1935]:437–464. Adam Parry describes these fragments as "extracts" (*MHV* [1971]:xxxix).

40. [M.] Parry *MHV* [1933–1935]:439.

41. See also Milman Parry's remarks in *MHV* [1928]:8–9, 20–21; [1928]:244; [1932]:326 n. 3.

not only ignored but even discounted by Adam Parry in his fifty-three-page introduction to his father's collected writings.[42] The son writes: "Meillet gave Parry confidence in following out his intuition that the structure of Homeric verse is altogether formulary; but he cannot be said to have vitally affected the direction of his thought."[43] Adam Parry's introduction slights not only the methodology of Meillet but also the comparative method in general, especially with reference to the comparative study of living South Slavic oral traditions.[44] The consequences are grave, because the readers of Milman Parry's collected writings have thus been predisposed, through the existing introduction by Adam Parry, to ignore the comparative aspects of the father's methodology.

There is also a far more basic problem here: the collected works of Milman Parry have been edited and published by his son instead of his student, Albert Lord. As a student of Lord, I can appreciate how radically different an introduction we would have if he had been the editor of his teacher's works. In such an introduction as written by Lord, readers would have been able to see clearly how his own work, as set forth in *The Singer of Tales* (1960), is a direct continuation of the work inaugurated by Milman Parry. The comparative aspects of Parry's methodology, which are more fully visible in Lord's work, would have been explained directly in terms of Parry's collected papers. In Adam Parry's existing introduction, by contrast, Lord's *The Singer of Tales* is presented not so much as a continuation but as a detour from *The Singer of Tales* that Milman Parry was planning to write when he died.[45]

It is only after reading thirty of the fifty-three pages of Adam Parry's introduction to his father's work that we find, finally, the first mention of Lord's book, *The Singer of Tales*.[46] Even here, the context is negative: Adam Parry goes out of his way to detach his father's work from Lord's and to attach it instead to the work of Classicists who resist the application of the comparative South Slavic evidence to Homer. Referring to the South Slavic oral traditions as simply an "analogy" used by both Parry and Lord in their study of Homer, he remarks: "To Lord, possibly even more than to Parry, the anal-

---

42. [A.] Parry *MHV* [1971]: ix–lxii.
43. Ibid.: xxiii.
44. For extensive documentation of the undervaluing of Meillet's methodology in Adam Parry's introduction, see Lamberterie 1997, esp. p. 7; also Mitchell and Nagy 2000: xvii.
45. See the negative remarks of Adam Parry in *MHV* [1971]: xxxvii n. 3, xlii n. 1, xliii n. 1, and, most overtly, xlviii (twice on this page). On the unfinished work of Milman Parry entitled *The Singer of Tales*, see the wording of Adam Parry *MHV* [1971]: xxxix, xli.
46. [A.] Parry *MHV* [1971]: xxxviii.

ogy is clear and certain."⁴⁷ Then, as an alternative to Lord's book, he refers
to "others" for whom "the analogy is far less sure," citing an article written by
himself and a book by G. S. Kirk.⁴⁸ These alternative works consistently undervalue the comparative methodology of Parry and Lord, which had been
founded on the central comparandum of the living South Slavic oral traditions that both of them had studied internally as well as comparatively. Further along in his introduction, Adam Parry sums up his own view: "Not the
slightest proof has yet appeared that the texts of the *Iliad* and *Odyssey* as we
have them, or any substantial connected portion of these texts, were composed by oral improvisation of the kind observed and described by Parry and
Lord and others in Jugoslavia and elsewhere."⁴⁹ He finds it "quite conceiv-
able" that "Homer made use of writing to compose a poem in a style which
had been developed by an oral tradition."⁵⁰

In short, the existing edition of Milman Parry's collected papers is framed
by an introduction that obscures the comparative aspects of his methodology
and even interferes with the continuation of that methodology in Albert
Lord's *The Singer of Tales*. For those Classicists who are inclined to resist the
applications of comparative methods, the introduction to *The Making of Homeric Verse* has made Homer "safe" again—or at least safe on the surface. So
long as Milman Parry is mediated by that introduction, he may even become
eligible for readmission among the ranks of such Classicists—provided he
stays separated from Albert Lord. Such an attitude on the part of a few Classicists does a disservice, I submit, to the whole field of Classics and detracts
from its humanism.⁵¹

Having observed such detours in the transmission of Parry's work, let us
now turn back to the basics, concerning the comparative methods shared by
Parry and Lord. Their methodology concentrated on the fundamentals of
(1) form and (2) content, in terms of (1) "formula" and (2) "theme" (smaller-
scale) or "type-scene" (larger-scale). Parry's collected papers (as published
finally in 1971) have more to say about "formula," while Lord's books (1960,

---

47. Ibid.
48. Ibid. The article is A. Parry 1966; the book is Kirk 1962. In note 1 of his introduction (*MHV*
[1971]:ix), Adam Parry acknowledges the advice of G. S. Kirk, among others—including Eric
Havelock and Hugh Lloyd-Jones. There is no mention of Albert Lord.
49. [A.] Parry *MHV* [1971]:lxi n. 1. On the problems created by the casual usage of the word
"improvisation," see *HQ* 26.
50. [A.] Parry *MHV* [1971]:lxi n. 1.
51. *HQ* 14.

1991, 1995) have more to say about "theme," but both are ultimately concerned with the same basic fact, that is, the actual interaction of formula and theme.[52] In comparing the existing text of Homeric poetry with the living oral traditions of South Slavic poetry, the ultimate test for the validity of comparison is this central question: Can we find parallelisms in the interaction of formula and theme? In the long run, it is the ongoing study of such interaction that vindicates the theory that Homeric poetry is indeed oral poetry.

Not only Lord but also Parry himself rigorously avoided speculating about the historical circumstances of Homeric poetry. The questions of why, how, when, and where the Homeric poems were recorded are left open by both Parry and Lord. This fact needs to be stressed, because there are those who appropriate to their own historical or linguistic reconstructions the legacy of Parry and Lord, as if these reconstructions were the be-all and end-all for such a legacy.

Of these four questions—why, how, when, and where the Homeric poems were recorded—Lord ventures to offer a tentative answer only about the "how," as he raises the possibility that the Homeric *Iliad* and *Odyssey* may have been dictated.[53] He does not pursue this possibility, however, beyond a purely comparative point of view, offering no opinions about why or when or where such a dictation might have taken place. In fact, he makes no judgments about the "how" of dictation, either. So we are still left, essentially, with all four questions unanswered: Why, how, when, and where were the Homeric poems recorded?

As I have already noted above in the introduction, Lord's general "dictation theory" was developed into various specific "dictation theories," notably by Janko, Jensen, and West; an extreme case is Powell.[54] Both Janko and Powell posit an eighth-century Homer for the dictation of both the *Iliad* and the *Odyssey*, while West and Jensen opt for the seventh and sixth centuries respectively, positing different historical circumstances. Each theory has different answers about why, how, when, and where. I have already expressed my disagreements with all these specific dictation theories, without opposing the more general dictation theory of Lord. Practically nothing in these spe-

---

52. Cf. *HQ* 18, 22–25.
53. Lord 1953, reprinted in Lord 1991, pp. 3–48, with an addendum.
54. Janko 1982:191, Jensen 1980:92, West 1990:34, Powell 1991:221–237. See introduction, "Question 3" above.

cific dictation theories, involving various elaborate historical or linguistic reconstructions, has to do directly with the methods of Parry and Lord, both of whom generally stayed away from arguments based on reconstructions.

The many disagreements growing out of the various dictation theories, which do not even agree among each other, have led to considerable confusion, at the moment of this writing, about the methodology of Parry and Lord in the field of Homeric studies. In the wake of all this confusion, it seemed to me essential to reaffirm in this book not only the methods but also the results of the work accomplished by Parry and Lord. Their results, like their methods, had practically nothing to do with the various dictation theories that are now in circulation.

I propose here to concentrate on the results. The evidentiary core of the legacy left behind by Parry and Lord is simply this: the Homeric text as we have it is comparable—on the levels of both form (formula) and content (theme/type-scene)—with what we observe in the recordings of living oral traditions, especially as collected in the historical context of the South Slavic traditions.

About this core of the Parry-Lord legacy there has been and continues to be general agreement even among the proponents of various specific "dictation theories." There is also general agreement about this core between the various dictation theorists and their opponents, such as myself. For example, my arguments in the book *Homeric Questions* (1996) about the "Parry-Lord theory" agree with almost all of the arguments in Janko's article about the same subject.[55] There is in general far more agreement than disagreement between Janko and myself.[56] Even if he and I disagree about the specifics of various historical and linguistic reconstructions, we agree basically about the evidentiary core, centering on the ongoing analysis of Homeric formulas, themes, and type-scenes.

The problem is that some proponents of the various specific "dictation theories" react to my disagreements with their historical or linguistic reconstructions by simply appropriating to themselves the general dictation theory of Lord, as if their theories were the inevitable extensions of Lord's. In this way, the dictation theory becomes a kind of shibboleth for determining ad-

---

55. Janko 1998b.
56. Janko's 1998b article and my 1996 book (*HQ*) mostly agree, even in our various disagreements with others.

herence to the methodology of Parry and Lord. An egregious pronouncer of such a shibboleth is Janko himself.[57]

Such rhetoric is pointless and even misleading, given that the theory of a dictating Homer is hardly a keystone of Lord's work, let alone Parry's. To repeat, Lord's formulation of a general "dictation theory" is purely comparative, and he makes no inferences about the historical background of Homer.

As for Parry, he never formulated any dictation theory of his own. Nevertheless, Janko extends his own theory of an orally dictated text of Homer, "which was absolutely fundamental to Albert Lord," to Milman Parry: "Indeed, Milman Parry never even considered any other explanation for the origin of the Homeric texts."[58] In support of this assertion, he cites an isolated remark of Parry, who wrote the following note to himself as he was preparing to put together his "Ćor Huso" project:

> I even figure to myself, just now, the moment when the author of the *Odyssey* sat and dictated his song, while another, with writing materials, wrote it down verse by verse, even in the way that our singers sit in the immobility of their thought, watching the motion of Nikola's hand across the empty page, when it will tell them it is the instant for them to speak the next verse.[59]

Parry did not develop this thought of his into a theory—or into an overall explanation for "the origin of the Homeric texts." Parry's linked thoughts, extending through the rest of the paragraph from which I have just quoted, need to be considered in their entirety. His next sentence, for example, reads: "The reasons I have for such an opinion are many, some of them still very vague, some very exact."[60] Then, on the next page of the printed version of Parry's informal notes to himself, a different but related dimension of his thinking emerges: "The whole problem of the transmission of the poems once composed is also one which must be considered in detail."[61]

Parry goes on to ponder "the alterations made to the Southslavic texts" by "unscholarly collectors and editors."[62] At this point in his thinking, he is un-

---

57. Janko 1998a, 1998b, 1998c.
58. Janko 1998a (no pagination).
59. [M.] Parry *MHV* [1971]: 451.
60. Ibid.
61. Ibid.: 452.
62. Ibid.

decided about the relevance of these South Slavic typologies to the history of the Homeric textual tradition, though he seems to be leaning in the direction of discounting the variants. He finishes by saying: "A methodological study along such lines will probably show us much about the sources of the variants of the texts such as Ludwich and Allen give them in their editions, about the longer and shorter papyrus texts, and the action of the early editors."[63]

In sum, though Parry entertained in one of his notes the idea of a dictating Homer, he also entertained alternative ideas in the same note and did not reach any conclusions. I stand by what I have already said elsewhere: Milman Parry never formulated a "dictation theory."[64]

My own answer concerning the whys, hows, whens, and wheres of Homeric poetry is reflected in my evolutionary model. This model, I must repeat, is not at odds with dictation models per se.

The differences between my evolutionary model and Janko's dictation model bring us back, one last time, to the question of irreversible mistakes in Homeric poetry. According to Janko's theory, an eighth-century Homeric dictation had left in its wake the vestiges of such mistakes in the Homeric textual tradition, which is supposedly the only direct line of continuity between Homer in the eighth century and our own text of Homer in the present.

I have already examined at length the two examples of Homeric "mistakes" that Janko adduces in his article on this subject.[65] Now let us turn to another example, in an earlier work of Janko.[66] It concerns *Iliad* 13.423, where a wounded warrior is described as 'groaning', στενάχοντα, even though we find in 13.402–423 that he has already died. In order to explain such an inconsistency, Janko invokes his theory that the Homeric *Iliad* was dictated in the eighth century B.C.E., which would be the point of origin for the "blunder" of στενάχοντα. For nearly half a millennium, according to this explanation, *Iliad* 13.402–423 happily coexisted, in a single textual tradition, with the version of 13.423 that featured στενάχοντα—until Aristarchus in the second century B.C.E. finally offered his "solution," reading στενάχοντε.[67]

---

63. Ibid. I have silently corrected "Ludwig" to "Ludwich."
64. Nagy 1997b (no pagination), Nagy 1998b (no pagination).
65. Janko 1998b.
66. Janko 1992: 99–100; also pp. 37–38.
67. On the formulaic integrity of this variant reading στενάχοντε adduced by Aristarchus, see below.

According to Janko, "such blunders decisively support Lord's view that the *Iliad* is an oral dictated text."[68] I have suggested instead that Lord's view is being used here and elsewhere to advance Janko's view—rather than the other way around.[69]

In fact, Lord's view is different in several ways from Janko's. To repeat, Lord does not speculate about a specific time (or place) for his heuristic model, which is essentially comparative in nature. Further, Lord's model is not based on the theory of an eighth-century Homer. Nor is it tied to theories of a textual transmission that somehow persists for several centuries without the possibility of any further significant contact with oral transmission. Nor does it depend on theories about Aristarchean "conjectures." For all these reasons and more, I resist Janko's identification of his model with that of Lord.[70]

From an evolutionary point of view, it would suffice to say in this case that *Iliad* 13.402–423 is incompatible with any version of 13.423 that features στενάχοντα instead of στενάχοντε, which is also textually attested. As I have argued elsewhere, both variants, στενάχοντα and στενάχοντε, are compatible with the formulaic system of Homeric poetry.[71]

I have already discussed at some length the implications of my evolutionary model for the making of Homeric poetry. For now, I concentrate on a single related question, which stems from an obvious fact. The fact is, Homeric poetry survives because it was written down. The basic question, then, is as obvious as the fact: What are the historical circumstances that led to the writing down of this poetry? The answer is elusive:

> As of now, no direct answer is available. Nor is there any consensus about why or how or even when Homeric poetry was written down. One thing and one thing only, it seems to me, is certain: no one has ever been able to prove that the technology of writing had been necessary for either the composition or the performance of Homeric poetry.[72]

This negative certainty about the writing down of the Homeric poems (by which I mean the *Iliad* and *Odyssey* combined) can be matched with a positive certainty about their composition: as I have stressed all along, Homeric

---

68. Janko 1992:99–100.
69. Nagy 1998b (no pagination).
70. This paragraph is excerpted from Nagy 1998b (no pagination).
71. Ibid. (no pagination).
72. *BA*² x–xi; cf. *HQ* 31.

poetry is a system. This system, moreover, can be explained consistently in terms of oral poetics. I have put it this way in my earlier work: "Homeric textual tradition is the primary evidence for this system, but it cannot be equated with the system itself."[73]

This last point is essential, I think, for a historical perspective on the genesis of the Homeric text as we know it. We must account not only for the text of Homer but also for the system as reflected by that text. I use the word "textualization" to express the idea of such a system. It is from this perspective that I developed my evolutionary model for the textualization of Homer, without presupposing that the actual composition of the "text" required the medium of writing:

> According to this [evolutionary] model, there were at least five distinct consecutive periods of Homeric oral/written transmission, "Five Ages of Homer," as it were, with each period showing progressively less fluidity and more rigidity. I argue that our Homeric text results from a "transcript tradition" that recorded the final or near-final stages in an evolving process of oral poetic recomposition-in-performance.[74]

Essential for the ultimate "textualization" of Homer is the Athenian era of Homeric poetry, that is, a sequence I describe as a combination of "period 3" (from the middle of the sixth century to the later part of the fourth) and "period 4" (from the later part of the fourth century to the second half of the second) in the "Five Ages of Homer." In this era, I argue for a decisive crystallization of the Homeric narratives of the *Iliad* and the *Odyssey* in the historical context of seasonally recurring performances by rhapsodes at the Festival of the Panathenaia. Metaphorically, I picture the Athenian or "Panathenaic" era of Homeric poetry as a bottleneck for the flow of ongoing oral traditions. In terms of this metaphor, the decentralized multiplicity of thematic and formal variants, typical of oral composition-in-performance as observed in the fieldwork of Parry and Lord, becomes gradually squeezed into a centralized unity that allows for only minimal variation. Here we see a major distinction between the *Iliad* and *Odyssey* on the one hand and, on the

---

73. *BA²* xi; cf. *PP* 107–152.

74. *BA²* xiv. See also the introduction above, "Question 2." See in general *PP* ch. 5 ("Multiform Epic and Aristarchus' Quest for the Real Homer"), ch. 6 ("Homer as Script"), and ch. 7 ("Homer as 'Scripture'"). On hermeneutic models of "transcript," see *PP* 110–113 and Bakker 1997:208 n. 3.

other, the archaic Greek epic traditions represented by the so-called Epic Cycle, namely, the *Cypria,* the *Aithiopis,* the *Little Iliad,* the *Iliou Persis,* and so on.[75] Only the *Iliad* and the *Odyssey* pass through the "Panathenaic Bottleneck," starting in the sixth century B.C.E.

The narrowing of the Homeric repertoire by way of Panathenaic centralization is correlative with a broadening of its appeal to an ever-wider public. The diffusion of a "Panathenaic Homer" is a model of centralization, not decentralization. In other words, there is more than one way to visualize the actual process of diffusion. Besides the pattern of an ever-widening radius of proliferation, with no clearly defined center of diffusion, there is also a more specialized pattern that is predicated on a functional center point, a centralized context for both the coming together of diverse audiences and the spreading outward of more unified traditions. A fixed center of diffusion can bring into play both centripetal and centrifugal forces. Such a center point is the seasonally recurring festival of the Panathenaia at Athens.[76]

The metaphor of the "Panathenaic Bottleneck" can be taken further. Tracing the evolution of Homeric poetry ahead in time, from the sixth century down to the second, I envision the neck of an upside-down bottle, already narrow in the sixth century, as it narrows even more in the era of Demetrius of Phalerum (317–307 B.C.E.), then widens somewhat in the era of the "eccentric papyri" (third century B.C.E.), and then finally narrows again in the era of Aristarchus (mid-second century B.C.E.), never to widen thereafter.[77]

In terms of an evolutionary model, it becomes unnecessary to posit any "irreversible mistakes" in Homeric poetry. Any mistakes in one performance can be corrected on the occasion of the next performance. Wherever changes happen in the course of an evolving oral poetic tradition, we may expect those changes to be systematically reinterpreted instead of being unsystematically misinterpreted.[78]

---

75. For important insights into the *Cypria,* see Burgess 1996, esp. 79–80. On the Epic Cycle in general, see Burgess 2001.

76. This paragraph is excerpted from *HQ* 43. Janko's (1998b:12) restatement of my diffusion model is not accurate (also, his cross-reference at p. 12 n. 66 to his n. 7 should be corrected to n. 18). Nor is he accurate in equating my model with the "memorial transmission" theory of Kirk 1962:88–98 and 1976:130–131. For my disagreement with Kirk's "devolutionary" model, see *HQ* 110–111.

77. For a prototype of this formulation, see *PP* 177–178. For more on the model represented by the metaphor of the "Panathenaic Bottleneck," see Nagy 2001a.

78. Further argumentation in Nagy 1997c:183.

Thus I resist the idea of a Homer who was nodding off at such dramatic moments as when the thunder of Zeus suddenly switches from a cloudy sky to a clear one, or when the dual forms of the Embassy Scene suddenly switch from situations requiring two characters to situations allowing three or more. I prefer the idea of a narrative plan that dares to call itself the Will of Zeus, and the god nods his assent in the positive sense of *neuō*, hardly in the negative sense of nodding off.

In the end I doubt that Homeric poetry, as performed by rhapsodes through the ages in the historical course of its ongoing reception in the Archaic and Classical periods and maybe even beyond, could ever have left its adoring audiences with any lasting impressions of irreversible mistakes committed by their prototypical poet, their very own divine Homer.

Chapter 4

The Shield of Achilles

Ends of the *Iliad* and Beginnings of the Polis

Homer critics have begun to interpret the resolution of the *Iliad* in Book 24, at the end of the epic, as a reflection of a new spirit that emerges from the heroic tradition and culminates in the ethos of the city-state or polis.[1] A sign of this ethos is the moment when Achilles, following his mother's instructions to accept compensation in the form of *apoina* 'ransom' offered by Priam for the killing of Patroklos by Hektor (*Iliad* 24.137), is finally moved to accept the ransom or *apoina* (24.502).[2] Consequently, he releases the corpse of Hektor for a proper funeral, thereby making possible his own heroic rehumanization.[3] I propose that the ethos leading toward a resolution at the end of the *Iliad* is already at work inside the very structure of the *Iliad*. Though the rules of Homeric poetry seem incompatible with overt references to the values of the polis, the poetry itself draws attention to this incompatibility in the timeless and even *limitless* picture of the City at War and the City at Peace, depicted in the hero's own microcosm, the Shield of Achilles, in *Iliad* 18.[4]

The original version of this essay is Nagy 1997a.

1. Seaford 1994, esp. p. 73, where the "narrative development" of the Iliadic ending is correlated with "the historical development of the polis." For narrative details reflecting the emerging institutions of the polis, cf. Scully 1990, esp. pp. 101–102.

2. My translation of *apoina* as 'ransom' follows the reasoning of Wilson 2002:9–11, 13–39.

3. Seaford 1994:69–71, 176–177; at p. 176, there is an important adjustment on the formulation of Macleod 1982:16 ("the value of humanity and fellow-feeling"). See also Crotty (1994), who argues that the ceremony of supplication that takes place in Book 24 of the *Iliad* creates an emotional effect so powerful—and so troubling—that it will take another epic, this time the *Odyssey*, to follow up on its resonances. For further refinements on the poetics of supplication in the *Iliad*, see Kim 2000, esp. pp. 18–34.

4. On the correspondences between depicted details on the Shield of Achilles and narrated details in the main narrative of the *Iliad*, see Taplin 1980. The detail that I am about to consider is not among the ones treated in that work. On the general topic of the poetics of ecphrasis in the Shield of Achilles passage, see Hubbard 1992 and Becker 1995. See also Stansbury-O'Donnell 1995

In describing this picture as "limitless," I have in mind an essay of Gotthold Ephraim Lessing, originally published in 1766, the title of which has been translated into English as *Laocoön: An Essay on the Limits of Painting and Poetry*. I draw attention not only to the use of the word "limits" in this title but also to the emphasis placed by Lessing on the "limitlessness" inherent in one particular detail of the picture, that is, a scene of a litigation that is taking place in the City at Peace.[5] In painting a picture through poetry, Lessing argues, the poet chooses not to confine himself to the limits of the art of making pictures. And yet, as we shall see, the picturing of this particular detail of a litigation allows "the poet" to go beyond the limits of his poetry as well. That is, the *Iliad* need not end where the linear narrative ends, to the extent that the pictures on the Shield of Achilles leave an opening into a virtual present, thus making the intent of the *Iliad* open-ended.[6]

Let us take a close look at this detail on the Shield of Achilles, picturing a litigation that is taking place in the City at Peace:

490 ἐν δὲ δύω ποίησε πόλεις μερόπων ἀνθρώπων
491 καλάς. ἐν τῇ μέν ῥα γάμοι τ' ἔσαν εἰλαπίναι τε.
492 νύμφας δ' ἐκ θαλάμων δαΐδων ὕπο λαμπομενάων
493 ἠγίνεον ἀνὰ ἄστυ, πολὺς δ' ὑμέναιος ὀρώρει·
494 κοῦροι δ' ὀρχηστῆρες ἐδίνεον, ἐν δ' ἄρα τοῖσιν
495 αὐλοὶ φόρμιγγές τε βοὴν ἔχον· αἱ δὲ γυναῖκες
496 ἱστάμεναι θαύμαζον ἐπὶ προθύροισιν ἑκάστη.
497 λαοὶ δ' εἰν ἀγορῇ ἔσαν ἀθρόοι· ἔνθα δὲ <u>νεῖκος</u>
498 ὠρώρει, δύο δ' ἄνδρες ἐνείκεον εἵνεκα <u>ποινῆς</u>
499 ἀνδρὸς ἀποφθιμένου· ὁ μὲν <u>εὔχετο</u> πάντ' ἀποδοῦναι
500 <u>δήμῳ</u> πιφαύσκων, ὁ δ' ἀναίνετο μηδὲν ἑλέσθαι·
501 ἄμφω δ' ἱέσθην ἐπὶ ἴστορι πεῖραρ ἑλέσθαι.
502 λαοὶ δ' ἀμφοτέροισιν ἐπήπυον ἀμφὶς ἀρωγοί·
503 κήρυκες δ' ἄρα <u>λαὸν</u> ἐρήτυον· οἱ δὲ γέροντες
504 εἵατ' ἐπὶ ξεστοῖσι λίθοις ἱερῷ ἐνὶ κύκλῳ,

---

for a wide-ranging critique of published interpretations concerning the composition of the Shield—from the standpoint of art history as well as literary history.

5. Lessing 1962 [1766]:ch. 19, pp. 99–100.

6. Cf. Hubbard 1992:17: "We do not see the shield as a finished product (for no man save Achilles can dare look upon it), but we see it in the process of fabrication by Hephaestus, as he adds ring after ring." Cf. Becker 1995:121; also Lynn-George 1988:49, 183–184 (whose valuable formulations will be discussed further below).

505 σκῆπτρα δὲ κηρύκων ἐν χέρσ' ἔχον ἠεροφώνων·
506 τοῖσιν ἔπειτ' ἤϊσσον. ἀμοιβηδὶς δὲ δίκαζον.
507 κεῖτο δ' ἄρ' ἐν μέσσοισι δύω χρυσοῖο τάλαντα,
508 τῷ δόμεν ὃς μετὰ τοῖσι δίκην ἰθύντατα εἴποι

490 On it he [= the divine smith Hephaistos] wrought two cities of mortal men.

491 And there were weddings in one, and feasts.

492 They were leading the brides along the city from their maiden chambers

493 under the flaring of torches, and the loud bride-song was arising.

494 The young men were dancing in circles, and among them

495 the pipes and the lyres kept up their clamor as in the meantime the women,

496 standing each at the door of the courtyard, admired them.

497 The people (*lāos*) were gathered together in the assembly place, and there a dispute (*neikos*)

498 had arisen, and two men were disputing (*neikeō*) about the blood-price (*poinē*)

499 for a man who had died (*apo-phthi-*). The one *made a claim* (*eukheto*) to pay back in full,

500 declaring publicly to the *district* (*dēmos*), but the other was refusing to accept anything.

501 Both were heading for an arbitrator (*histōr*), to get a limit (*peirar*);

502 and the people (*lāos*) were speaking up on either side, to help both men.

503 But the heralds kept the people (*lāos*) in hand, as meanwhile elders

504 were seated on benches of polished stone in a sacred (*hieros*) circle

505 and took hold in their hands of scepters (*skēptron*) from the heralds who lift their voices.

506 And with these they sprang up, taking turns, and rendered their judgments (*dik-azō*),[7]

507 and in their midst lay on the ground two weights of gold,

508 to be given to the one among them who pronounced a judgment (*dikē*) most correctly.

Iliad 18.490–508

---

7. On the juridical background for the notion that a speaker is authorized to speak by holding a *skēptron*, see Easterling 1989:106, with specific reference to this passage in *Iliad* 18.

This juridical scene, I propose, lays the conceptual foundations for the beginnings of the polis, even though the telling of the scene itself is framed by an epic medium that pretends, as it were, that there is as yet no polis.[8] Despite this pretense, the existence of the polis is indirectly acknowledged in the image of an inner circle of elders surrounding the scene, debating the rights and the wrongs played out in the juridical proceedings, and in the image of an outer circle made up of people who voice their approval or disapproval of the elders' formulations, thereby deciding who is to win the prize placed at the center of the proceedings, the two weights of gold (18.506–508).[9]

Of special importance to me is the research of Leonard Muellner on this passage.[10] Muellner studies the use of *eukhomai* in *Iliad* 18.499, a verse from the passage quoted above, and he stresses that this verse contains the only overt literary attestation of this word in a juridical context—a context confirmed by the evidence of the Linear B tablets. He notes the reference to a juridical procedure in one of these tablets:

Text as transliterated from the Linear B syllabic script
e-ri-ta i-je-re-ja e-ke
e-u-ke-to-qe e-to-ni-jo e-ke-e
te-o da-mo-de-mi pa-si ko-to-na-o
ke-ke-me-na-o o-na-to e-ke-e

Greek text as reconstructed from the syllabic script[11]
e-ri-ta hiereia ekhei
eukhetoi-k^w e e-to-ni-jo ekheen
theōi; dāmos de min phāsi ktoināōn
kekeimenāōn onāton ekheen

Translation
e-ri-ta the priestess has
and makes a claim (*eukhetoi-k^w e*) to have *e-to-ni-jo*-land

---

8. Cf. Seaford 1994:25: "The world on the shield seems to represent the everyday life of the audience, including a city at peace, as a contrast to the heroic world of the main narrative, in which there is no judicial mechanism to resolve the crisis of reciprocity."

9. Cf. Edwards 1991:214, 218; for analogies to this description of early Greek law in early Germanic law, see Wolff 1946, esp. pp. 44–46. For more on the litigation scene, see also Hubbard 1992:29–30, Becker 1995:119–123.

10. Muellner 1976:100–106.

11. Where the reconstruction is uncertain, I leave the text as transliterated from the syllabic script.

on behalf of the god; but the *dāmos* says that she has, from the land holdings [= *ktoinai*]

that are common,[12] a holding-in-usufruct [= *onāton*].

Pylos tablet Ep 704

Let us review the corresponding words in the *Iliad* 18 passage quoted above:

497   The people (*lāos*) were gathered together in the assembly place, and there a dispute (*neikos*)

498   had arisen, and two men were disputing (*neikeō*) about the blood-price (*poinē*)

499   for a man who had died (*apo-phthi-*). The one made a claim (*eukheto*) to pay back in full,

500   declaring publicly to the district (*dēmos*), but the other was refusing to accept anything.

I repeat, Muellner stresses that this Homeric passage is the only overt literary attestation, in all of Greek literature, where this word is found in a juridical context—a context confirmed by the evidence of the Linear B tablets.

Following Muellner's analysis, Raymond Westbrook published an article analyzing Near Eastern parallels to the evidence of the Homeric and the Linear B juridical contexts.[13] Also, he made an adjustment to Muellner's interpretation of the Linear B text (the translation that I have just given reflects this change), and, by extension, of the Homeric text as well. Westbrook points out that the priestess mentioned in the Linear B tablet may be making a claim to the *right* of landholding, not necessarily to the *fact* of landholding.[14] Let us look at the wording again:

e-ri-ta the priestess has

and makes a claim (*eukhetoi-k^{w}e*) to have *e-to-ni-jo*-land

on behalf of the god; but the *dāmos* says that she has, from the landholdings (= *ktoinai*)

that are common, a holding-in-usufruct (= *onāton*).

---

12. Hooker (1980:139) thinks that *ke-ke-me-na ko-to-na* is common land "leased" from the *dāmos*.

13. Westbrook 1992.

14. Ibid.: 73–74.

By extension, Westbrook argues that the defendant in the scene of litigation on the Shield of Achilles is likewise claiming the *right* to pay compensation in the form of *poinē*—that is, reparation in full—for the death of the man mentioned in verse 499 of *Iliad* 18. Let us look at the wording again:

499   The one made a claim (*eukheto*) to pay back in full,
500   declaring publicly to the district (*dēmos*), but the other was refusing
         to accept anything.

Presumably the defense contends that the man did not die as a result of aggravated murder, and that there were mitigating circumstances. Comparing the evidence of analogous Near Eastern juridical documents, Westbrook postulates "(a) that the ransom would be fixed by the court, in accordance with the objective criteria of traditional law," and "(b) that the basis for such a claim by the killer would be that the case is one of mitigated homicide."[15]

In making his arguments, Westbrook adduces a variety of parallels, from which I select the following:

1. He notes in general: "With homicide and other serious crimes, the court determined not only the facts of the case but also the legal questions: (a) whether the plaintiff was entitled to revenge at all, and (b) the appropriate revenge *or* ransom to which the plaintiff was entitled."[16]
2. Hittite Edict of King Telepinu 49: "A matter of blood is as follows. Whoever does blood, whatever *the owner of the blood* says. If he says, 'Let him die!' he shall die. If he says, 'Let him pay ransom!' he shall pay ransom. But to the king, nothing."[17]
3. Neo-Assyrian legal document (ADD 321): "{A} the son of {B} shall give {C}, daughter of {D}, the scribe, in lieu of the blood. He shall wash the blood. If {A} does not give the woman, they will kill him on {B}'s grave. Whichever of them breaks the contract shall pay ten mina of silver."[18] We may compare the two weights of gold in the Iliadic picture of the Shield, verses 507 to 508 in the passage quoted above.[19]

---

15. Ibid.: 74.
16. Ibid.: 58.
17. Translation after ibid.: 57; highlighting mine.
18. Translation after ibid.: 58.
19. As we shall see later, however, the ultimate winner of the gold in *Iliad* 18.507–508 turns out to be neither of the litigants. On the two weights in gold, see also the discussion of Stansbury-O'Donnell 1995:323.

4. Arguing against the notion of *Erfolgshaftung,* that is, strict liability, West-brook suggests that there was "some gradation of homicide based on the mental condition of the offender."[20]

5. Codex Hammu-rabi 206–207: "If a man strikes a man in a brawl and inflicts a wound on him, the man shall swear 'I did not strike knowingly' and he shall pay the doctor. If he dies from being struck, he shall swear, and if it was the son of a man, he shall pay half a mina of silver."[21] Again we may compare the two weights of gold in the Iliadic picture of the Shield, verses 507 to 508 in the passage quoted above.

6. *Iliad* 23.86–90, Patroklos recalls how, as a boy, he fled his homeland be-cause he had killed another boy over a game of dice, *ouk ethelōn* 'not willingly' but *kholōtheis* 'in anger'. Westbrook compares the parallel for-mulation in Near Eastern law codes where one person kills another "not knowingly." He infers: "There must be two elements in mitigation, a threshold situation for which the killer was not entirely to blame, i.e., a fight or a quarrel in which he was provoked, and lack of intention to strike a fatal blow."[22]

7. With regard to the litigation scene in the City at Peace, Westbrook con-cludes: "The reason why the killer and not the other party is said to be ar-guing before this court is that *the burden of proof is upon him* to establish the existence of *mitigating circumstances,* as we have seen from our discus-sion of the Near Eastern sources. The other party, the avenger, has the dual right to ransom *or* revenge. By refusing to take ransom, he asserts that the case is one of aggravated homicide and he therefore has a free choice between ransom and revenge, and chooses the latter."[23]

In short, following Westbrook, I think that the rationale of the litigation scene on Achilles' Shield is basically this: the defendant wishes the limit to be ransom, not revenge, while the plaintiff wishes the limit to be revenge, not ransom.[24] I draw attention to my use of the word *limit,* which corresponds to the juridical sense that we are about to examine in *Iliad* 18.501, in the picture of the litigation scene in the City at Peace. In what follows I shall try to con-

---

20. Westbrook 1992:73.
21. Translation after ibid.: 61–62.
22. Ibid.: 71.
23. Ibid.: 75.
24. Ibid.: 75–76.

nect a juridical sense of limits with a poetic sense of limits, in pursuing my general argument that the picture of the litigation scene allows "the poet" to go beyond the limits of his poetry.

Let us take an even closer look at the litigation scene in the City at Peace:

497   The people (*lāos*) were gathered together in the assembly place, and
       there a dispute (*neikos*)
498   had arisen, and two men were disputing (*neikeō*) about the blood-
       price (*poinē*)
499   for a man who had died (*apo-phthi-*). The one made a claim
       (*eukheto*) to pay back in full,
500   declaring publicly to the district (*dēmos*), but the other was refusing
       to accept anything.
501   Both were heading for an arbitrator (*histōr*), to get a limit.

Iliad 18.497–501

The defendant is expounding his case to the *dēmos*, as we see from line 500, and Leonard Muellner makes it clear that the same word, *dāmos*, which must be interpreted as 'district' or 'community', functions in the Linear B documents as a legal entity in its own right.[25] Westbrook finds this step in Muellner's argument crucial.[26] I should add that Muellner's argument here is strengthened by the methodology that he applies to his detailed analysis, which combines historical linguistics as perfected by Antoine Meillet and Emile Benveniste with formulaic analysis as pioneered by Milman Parry and Albert Lord. Muellner stresses that Michel Lejeune, another historical linguist, defines the *dāmos* in the Linear B tablets as an administrative entity endowed with a juridical function.[27] In other words, the *dāmos* can be seen as a prototype of the polis.[28]

In the light of Muellner's work, as mediated by Westbrook, verses 499–500 of *Iliad* 18 can be interpreted as follows: "The one man was claiming [to be able, to have a right] to pay everything [i.e., to be free of other penalties], the other refused to accept anything [i.e., any pecuniary recompense in place

---

25. Muellner 1976:104.
26. Westbrook 1992:67.
27. Muellner 1976:104, citing Lejeune 1965:12.
28. Cf. *PH* 251 n. 10.

of the exile or death of the offender]." [29] Westbrook's own work can be summarized thus:

> Westbrook therefore holds that in this trial scene the killer is claiming the right to pay ransom (*poinē*, 498) in full (*panta*, 499) on the grounds of mitigated homicide, the amount to be fixed by the court. The other party is claiming and choosing the right to the revenge, as in cases of aggravated homicide. The court must set the 'limit' (*peirar*, 501) of the penalty, i.e., whether it should be revenge or ransom and also the appropriate 'limit' of either revenge or ransom. [30]

Again I focus on the word *peirar* 'limit' at verse 501 of the Shield passage. This reference to the 'limit' of the case is relevant to the visualization of an inner circle of elders who are attempting to define such limits—and of an outer circle of people who are in turn attempting to define the best definition of such limits. In terms of a linear narrative, the *peirata* or 'limits' of the *Iliad* would be the end of the *Iliad*, when Achilles finally accepts compensation in the form of *apoina*, that is, ransom. In terms of the concentric circles that surround the scene of litigation in the Shield of Achilles, on the other hand, the *peirata* or 'limits' are pushed to the outermost limits of the *Iliad*, that is, to the broadest possible interpretive community.

I shall return in a moment to this notion of a broadest-based audience for the *Iliad*. The emphasis for now, however, is on the *peirata* or 'limits' of the litigation in the Shield of Achilles passage. Here it is also relevant to ask whether the claim of the defendant at *Iliad* 18.499 is a *fact* of paying rather than a *right* to pay. [31] Such a question, however, does not affect Muellner's overall interpretation, which goes beyond the immediate context of the two litigants on the Shield—and which certainly goes beyond the objectives of those who stress simply the juridical force of both the Linear B and the Homeric *eukhomai*. [32] As Muellner says clearly about the context of *eukhomai* at 18.499, "The issue is not whether the fine was actually paid." [33] Rather, as he

---

29. Edwards 1991:215.
30. Ibid.: 216.
31. Ibid.: 215, citing Perpillou (1970:537), who cites the evidence of Linear B *eukhomai* and who translates the Homeric *eukhomai* at 18.499 in terms of the defendant's claiming a *right*, not a *fact*. Westbrook (1992) did not use the work of Perpillou.
32. Perpillou 1970:537.
33. Muellner 1976:106.

makes it quite clear, the issue is whether the plaintiff is morally obliged to accept the payment.

It is in this context that Muellner cites the words of Ajax to Achilles in *Iliad* 9:[34]

νηλής· καὶ μέν τίς τε κασιγνήτοιο φονῆος
ποινὴν ἢ οὗ παιδὸς ἐδέξατο τεθνηῶτος·
καί ῥ' ὁ μὲν ἐν δήμῳ μένει αὐτοῦ πόλλ' ἀποτίσας.
τοῦ δέ τ' ἐρητύεται κραδίη καὶ θυμὸς ἀγήνωρ
ποινὴν δεξαμένῳ· σοὶ δ' ἄλληκτόν τε κακόν τε
θυμὸν ἐνὶ στήθεσσι θεοὶ θέσαν εἵνεκα κούρης
οἵης.

Pitiless one! A man accepts from the slayer of his brother
a blood-price (*poinē*), or for a son that has died;
and the slayer remains in his own district (*dēmos*), paying a great price,
and his [= the kinsman's] heart and proud spirit are restrained
once he accepts the blood-price (*poinē*). But for you it was an implacable and bad
spirit that the gods put in your breast, for the sake of a girl
—just one single girl!

Iliad 9.632–638

We may compare the wording in the Shield passage:

499   for a man who had died (*apo-phthi-*). The one made a claim
      (*eukheto*) to pay back in full,
500   declaring publicly to the district (*dēmos*), but the other was refusing
      to accept anything.

Iliad 18.499–500

This passage in *Iliad* 18 has been compared to the *Iliad* 9 passage quoting the words of Ajax concerning the hypothetical acceptance of *poinē* and to the *Iliad* 24 passage concerning the actual acceptance of *apoina* by Achilles at the end of the *Iliad* (24.137, 502).[35] Here I must note a problem in some of the in-

---

34. Ibid.
35. Muellner 1976 and Andersen 1976. Cf. Edwards (1991:216), who cites the second of these publications but not the first.

terpretations of the litigation passage. In the words of Keith Stanley, some interpreters go "against strict design."[36] By this, Stanley means that some interpreters find the *Iliad* 9 passage—as also the *Iliad* 24 passage—useful for understanding the *Iliad* 18 passage concerning the litigation, but not necessarily the other way around.

For Muellner, by contrast, the relationship between the outer world of the overall narrative and the inner world of the Shield, in particular the litigation scene, is not a matter of one-way communication: rather, the communication goes both ways.[37] Muellner's interpretation applies the insights of I. A. Richards in his study of similes.[38] Richards uses the term "tenor" for any framing structure, such as a narrative, and the term "vehicle" for the simile as an inner structure that is framed by an outer structure. For Richards, as for Muellner, the communication between the *tenor* or the framing structure and the *vehicle* or the framed structure is not one way but both ways.

Just as the logic of a simile spills over into the logic of the narrative frame, so also the logic of the story-within-a-story, the litigation scene, spills over into the logic of the story of Achilles, affecting all other passages. From Muellner's point of view, you cannot say that you have "solved" the meaning of the litigation scene if you disregard its relation to the main narrative.

From the standpoint of the *Iliad* as a linear progression, there is a sense of closure as the main narrative comes to an end in Book 24. From the standpoint of the Shield passage, however, the *Iliad* is open-ended. In other words, the vehicle reopens the tenor. In order to make this argument, I must first confront a paradox: the world as represented on the Shield seems to be closed and unchanging, as opposed to the openness of the *Iliad* to changes that happen to the figures in the story *while the story is in progress*. The question is, however, What happens when the story draws to a close? Now the figures inside the *Iliad* become frozen into their actions by the finality of what has been narrated. This freezing is completed once all is said and done, at the precise moment when the whole story has been told. This moment, which is purely notional from the standpoint of Iliadic composition, gets captured by the

---

36. Stanley 1993:309, with specific reference to Andersen 1976. There is a similar problem with the interpretation of Edwards 1991:213.

37. Muellner 1976:106.

38. Richards 1936.

frozen motion-picture of the Shield. Time has now stopped still, and the open-endedness of contemplating the artistic creation can begin.

The case in point is the scene of the litigants in the City at Peace: Muellner argues that the syntax of *mēden* 'nothing' at *Iliad* 18.500 makes it explicit that the miniature plaintiff in the picture will absolutely never accept any compensation.[39] Such a notional moment must be distinguished, however, from the real moments of the narrative in progress: later, in Book 19, soon after the description of the Shield, Achilles himself will be offered gifts from Agamemnon, which the king had intended as compensation in the form of *apoina* 'ransom' for the loss of Briseis.[40] Still later, in Book 24, Achilles will accept the *apoina* 'ransom' offered by Priam as compensation for the death of Patroklos. And yet, from the synoptic standpoint of the *Iliad* writ large, as it were, Achilles remains utterly inflexible in refusing compensation—for the ultimate loss of his own life.[41]

In order to pursue this point, I focus on an instance of textual variation at *Iliad* 18.499 between *apophthimenou* 'a man who died' and *apoktamenou* 'a man who was killed'. The second variant, as we learn from the scholia, was noted by Zenodotus. If indeed the Shield passage, as a vehicle, can refer to the main narrative of the *Iliad* as the tenor, then the referent of this variant *apoktamenou* can be Patroklos, as suggested by *Iliad* 24, where Achilles accepts the *apoina* or compensation from Hektor's father Priam for the death of Patroklos.

I use the word "referent" here in a diachronic sense, that is, viewing various different degrees of cross-referencing in Homeric composition. It is from

---

39. Muellner 1976:106. Wilson (2002:161) agrees, adding this adjustment: what the plaintiff will never accept is "composition," that is, payment in prestige goods. The plaintiff reserves the right to exact *tisis*, that is, payment in harm (ibid.: 39).

40. My formulation here is based on my earlier wording in *PH* 254, with an adjustment added in the light of the insights of Wilson 2002. Wilson argues convincingly that Achilles refuses to think of Agamemnon's gifts as *apoina* 'ransom'. See Wilson 2002:10: "Although Achilleus feels he is owed *poinē* [revenge] for the seizure of Briseis, Agamemnon offers him *apoina* [ransom]." See also ibid.: 87: "When Achilleus redefines the seizure of Briseis as loss of a bride (*alokhos thmarēs*, 9.337), he puts her in a familial relationship to himself and, as a result, transfers her from the sphere of prestige goods to that of persons, and, more to the point, family." For a most perceptive analysis of the role of Briseis in the Homeric *Iliad*, see Dué 2002.

41. Wilson (2002:202 n. 97) says: "I find my point that Achilleus ultimately seeks compensation for his own life independently confirmed by Nagy (1997[d]) 204." The page cited by Wilson contains the same point as rewritten here. On this point, I disagree with the reasoning of Lowenstam 1993:100 n. 103 (citing Andersen 1976:16).

a diachronic perspective that I find it useful to consider the phenomenon of Homeric cross-references, especially long-distance ones that happen to reach for hundreds or even thousands of lines: here it is important to stress again that any such cross-reference that we admire in our two-dimensional text did not just happen one time in one performance—but presumably countless times in countless reperformances within the three-dimensional continuum of a specialized oral tradition. The resonances of Homeric cross-referencing must be appreciated within the larger context of a long history of repeated performances.[42]

If Patroklos is the referent of *apoktamenou* 'a man who was killed', the variant in *Iliad* 18.499, then there may be an ulterior meaning in the Ajax speech in *Iliad* 9: Achilles is justified in refusing compensation in the form of *apoina* 'ransom' offered by Agamemnon in the Embassy Scene of *Iliad* 9 because, in the long run, the compensation in question also concerns the death of Patroklos, not only the loss of Briseis.[43] In the long run, Agamemnon has a share in causing the death of Patroklos and is to that extent liable. Such liability could be viewed, outside the story, as an alternative motivation for his offer of compensation in the form of *apoina*.

In the longer run, however, it was Achilles himself who caused the death of Patroklos, since he could not in good conscience accept the *apoina* 'ransom' offered by Agamemnon as compensation for Briseis—and since Patroklos consequently took the place of Achilles in battle.[44] In the longer run, then, Achilles can be a defendant as well as a plaintiff in litigation over the death of Patroklos.[45] In the longest run, though, Achilles can even be the victim himself, since the *Iliad* makes his own death a direct consequence of the death of Patroklos.[46] No wonder the plaintiff of the Shield scene will not accept compensation in the form of *poinē*: potentially, he is also the defendant, and even the victim! In this light, it becomes more difficult for the narrative to say that *anyone* is liable for killing Achilles. It becomes easier now to think of the hero not specifically as *apoktamenou* 'a man who was killed', but more generally as *apophthimenou* 'a man who died'.

---

42. This paragraph repeats what I said in *HQ* 82.
43. Cf. *PH* 253–255.
44. *PH* 254 n. 29, esp. with reference to *Iliad* 9.502–512.
45. *BA* 109–110, 312. Here I find it useful to invoke the Near Eastern concept of a "split legal personality," as discussed by Wilson 2002:198 n. 25.
46. *PH* 254.

Earlier, I made the claim that, just as the logic of a simile spills over into the logic of the narrative frame, so also the logic of the story-within-a-story, the litigation scene, spills over into the logic of the story of Achilles. But there is more to it: it spills over even further, into the logic of the audience that responds to the overall story. Moreover, the logic of the audience can loop back to the logic of the original litigation scene. It is an endless coming-full-circle, an endlessly self-renewing cycle.

In order to comprehend how this logic comes full circle, I propose to rethink the litigation scene, one more time, all over again. In this litigation, the immediate response is to come from an inner circle of supposedly impartial elder adjudicators who compete with each other about who can best define the rights and wrongs of the case. In the inner world of the Shield of Achilles, this group of arbitrators must compete with each other in rendering justice, until one winning solution can at last be found. Such a winning solution is also needed for the *Iliad* as a whole, which does not formally take a position on the question "Who is *aitios* 'guilty, responsible' in the narrative?" The response to this question is left up to someone beyond the *Iliad*.

Within the *Iliad*, in the inner world of the Shield, there is a point of contact with that someone: it is the *histōr* 'arbitrator' at verse 501. He is the one whose function it is to render the most righteous *dikē* 'judgment'. Within the *Iliad*, in the inner world of the Shield of Achilles, the ultimate winner in the competition among the inner circle of elders is to be that special someone—that single *histōr* 'arbitrator' who will at last respond to the central question of the litigation by formulating the most righteous *dikē* 'judgment'.[47]

For the winner of the competition among this inner circle of elders, the immediate prize is the gold, two weights of it, highlighted in verses 507 and 508 of the litigation scene. This gold is the visual focal point of the competition, in which the ultimate winner is the one who takes all, and this winner is neither of the two litigants. The two weights of this gold, balancing the claims of the two litigants, will go instead to that special someone who gives the perfect response to the central question of the litigation.

But then the question is, How fitting a prize is this gold for that special someone? The response is open-ended. The logic of the litigation scene is not self-contained, since it reaches beyond the inner circle of supposedly im-

---

47. This formulation builds on the observations in *PH* 255.

partial elder adjudicators who compete over the perfect definition of the rights and wrongs of the case. The inner logic of the inner circle spills over into the outer logic of an outer circle of people who surround the elders, the people who are waiting to hear the elders' definitions and who will then define who defines most justly. Moreover, as Michael Lynn-George notices, that defining voice is an end that is anticipated but "is always still to come."[48] Lynn-George continues: "The process is a desire for a finality that is infinitely deferred."[49] In the end, then, the inner logic of the litigation scene spills over, paradoxically, into the outer logic of an ever-expanding outermost circle, that is, people who are about to hear the *Iliad.* From a historical point of view, that audience is the people of the polis.

I started by saying that the logic of this outermost circle—of the audience that responds to the overall story—loops back to the logic of the innermost circle, of the litigants in the original litigation scene. By way of this looping back, the responses to the questions posed by the innermost circle become externally relativized, even if the responses of Homeric poetry are internally absolutized by its self-equation with mantic poetry. The value of the two weights of gold becomes no longer absolute, but relative.

The idea of a relativized *Iliad,* the limits of which are delimited, paradoxically, by the expanding outermost circle of an ever-evolving polis outside the narrative, is compatible with a historical view of Homeric poetry as an open-ended and ever-evolving process. Earlier, I described this view of Homer in terms of an evolutionary model. Such an evolutionary model cannot be pinned down, I argued, to any single "Age of Homer." I suggested that we need not think of any single age of Homer, but rather, several ages of Homer.

This evolutionary model is the lens through which I see the picture on the Shield of Achilles, with its concentric circles of limits expanding further and further outward.[50] I repeat what I said earlier, this time going one step further. The logic of the litigation scene spills over into the logic of a surrounding circle of supposedly impartial elder adjudicators who are supposed to define the rights and wrongs of the case. Next, the logic of this inner circle

---

48. Lynn-George 1988:183.

49. Ibid.: 184.

50. In terms of an evolutionary model, I suggest that the variant noted by Zenodotus at *Iliad* 18.499, *apoktamenou* 'a man who was killed' instead of *apophthimenou* 'a man who died', reflects a relatively earlier version of Iliadic narrative.

of elders spills over into the logic of an outer circle of people who surround the elders, the people who will define who defines most justly. Next, it spills over into the logic of the outermost circle, people who are about to hear the *Iliad*. These people who hear Homeric poetry, as I said, are to become the people of the polis. Going one step further, these people are even ourselves.

Bibliography

Andersen, Ø. 1976. "Some Thoughts on the Shield of Achilles." *Symbolae Osloenses* 51:5–18.

Austin, N. 1975. *Archery at the Dark of the Moon: Poetic Problems in Homer's* Odyssey. Berkeley and Los Angeles.

———. 1991. "The Wedding Text in Homer's *Odyssey*." *Arion* 3d ser., 1:227–243.

Bakker, E. J. 1997. *Poetry in Speech: Orality and Homeric Discourse.* Ithaca, N.Y.

Becker, A. S. 1995. *The Shield of Achilles and the Poetics of Ekphrasis.* Lanham, Md.

Broggiato, M. 1998. "Cratete di Mallo negli Scholl. A ad *Il.* 24.282 e ad *Il.* 9.169a." *Seminari Romani Di Cultura Greca* 1:137–143.

Burgess, J. S. 1996. "The Non-Homeric *Cypria*." *Transactions of the American Philological Association* 126:77–99.

———. 2001. *The Tradition of the Trojan War in Homer and the Epic Cycle.* Baltimore.

Carter, J. B., and S. P. Morris, eds. 1995. *The Ages of Homer: A Tribute to Emily Townsend Vermeule.* Austin.

Clarke, M. 1999. *Flesh and Spirit in the Songs of Homer: A Study of Words and Myths.* Oxford.

Clay, J. S. 1983. *The Wrath of Athena: Gods and Men in the* Odyssey. Princeton. [2d ed., 1997, Lanham, Md.]

Crotty, K. 1994. *The Poetics of Supplication: Homer's* Iliad *and* Odyssey. Ithaca, N.Y.

Davidson, O. M. 2000. *Comparative Literature and Classical Persian Poetics.* Costa Mesa, Calif.

Day, J. W. 1989. "Rituals in Stone: Early Greek Grave Epigrams and Monuments." *Journal of Hellenic Studies* 109:16–28.

Denniston, J. D. 1954. *The Greek Particles.* 2d ed., revised by K. J. Dover. Oxford.

Dougherty, C. 2001. *The Raft of Odysseus: The Ethnographic Imagination of Homer's* Odyssey. Oxford.

Dué, C. 2002. *Homeric Variations on a Lament by Briseis.* Lanham, Md.

Dumézil, G. 1984. ". . . *Le moyne noir en gris dedans Varennes.*" Paris.

———. 1999. *The Riddle of Nostradamus: A Critical Dialogue.* Translation by B. Wing from Dumézil 1984. Baltimore.

Dunkel, G. 1979. "Fighting Words: Alcman *Partheneion* 63, *makhontai.*" *Journal of Indo-European Studies* 7:249–272.

Easterling, P. E. 1989. "Agamemnon's *skēptron* in the *Iliad*." In *Images of Authority: Papers Presented to Joyce Reynolds on the Occasion of Her Seventieth Birthday,* edited by M. M. Mackenzie and C. Roueché, Cambridge Philological Society, suppl. vol. 16, 104–121. Cambridge.

Edwards, A. T. 1988. "ΚΛΕΟΣ ΑΦΘΙΤΟΝ and Oral Theory." *Classical Quarterly* 38:25–30.

Edwards, M. W., ed. 1991. *The* Iliad: *A Commentary*. Vol. 5. General Ed. G. S. Kirk. Cambridge.

Flueckiger, J. B. 1996. *Gender and Genre in the Folklore of Middle India*. Ithaca, N.Y.

Foley, J. M., ed. 1981. *Oral Traditional Literature: A Festschrift for Albert Bates Lord*. Columbus, Ohio.

———. 1991. *Immanent Art: From Structure to Meaning in Traditional Oral Epic*. Bloomington, Ind.

Ford, A. 1992. *Homer: The Poetry of the Past*. Ithaca, N.Y.

Fowler, R. 1983. Review of Nagy 1979. *Echos du monde classique/Classical Views*, n.s. 2:117–129.

Goldhill, S. 1996. Review of Olson 1995. *Classical Philology* 91:180–184.

Guillén, C. 1985. *Entre lo uno y lo diverso: Introducción a la literatura comparada*. Barcelona.

———. 1993. *The Challenge of Comparative Literature*. Translation by C. Franzen of Guillén 1985. Harvard Studies in Comparative Literature 42. Cambridge, Mass.

Habinek, T. 1998. "Singing, Speaking, Making, Writing: Classical Alternatives to Literature and Literary Studies." *Stanford Humanities Review* 6:65–75.

Hainsworth, J. B. 1988. Commentary on Books v–viii of the *Odyssey*. In A. Heubeck, S. West, and J. B. Hainsworth, eds., *A Commentary on Homer's* Odyssey. Oxford.

Hooker, J. T. 1980. *Linear B: An Introduction*. Bristol.

Householder, F. W., and G. Nagy. 1972. *Greek: A Survey of Recent Work*. The Hague.

Hubbard, T. K. 1992. "Nature and Art in the Shield of Achilles." *Arion*, 3d ser., 2:16–41.

Jacopin, P.-Y. 1988. "Anthropological Dialectics: Yukuna Ritual as Defensive Strategy." *Schweizerische Amerikanisten-Gesellschaft, Bulletin* 52:35–46.

Janko, R. 1982. *Homer, Hesiod and the Hymns: Diachronic Development in Epic Diction*. Cambridge.

———. 1992. *The* Iliad: *A Commentary*. Vol. 4. General ed. G. S. Kirk. Cambridge.

———. 1998a. Review of Morris and Powell 1997. *Bryn Mawr Classical Review* 98.5.20.

———. 1998b. "The Homeric Poems as Oral Dictated Texts." *Classical Quarterly* 48:1–13.

———. 1998c. Review of Nagy 1996a. *Journal of Hellenic Studies* 118:206–207.

Jensen, M. Skafte. 1980. *The Homeric Question and the Oral-Formulaic Theory*. Copenhagen.

Kazazis, J. N., and A. Rengakos, eds. 1999. *Euphrosyne: Studies in Ancient Epic and Its Legacy in Honor of Dimitris N. Maronitis*. Stuttgart.

Kim, J. 2000. *The Pity of Achilles: Oral Style and the Unity of the* Iliad. Lanham, Md.

Kirk, G. S. 1962. *The Songs of Homer*. Cambridge.

————. 1976. *Homer and the Oral Tradition.* Cambridge.

Koller, H. 1957. "Hypokrisis und Hypokrites." *Museum Helveticum* 14:100–107.

Lamberterie, C. de. 1997. "Milman Parry et Antoine Meillet." In Létoublon 1997:9–22. Translated as "Milman Parry and Antoine Meillet," in Loraux, Nagy, and Slatkin 2001:409–421.

Langdon, S., ed. 1997. *New Light on a Dark Age: Exploring the Culture of Geometric Greece.* Columbia, Mo.

Lejeune, M. 1965. "Le ΔΑΜΟΣ dans la société mycénienne." *Revue des etudes grecques* 78:1–22.

Lessing, G. E. 1962 [1766]. *Laocoön: An Essay on the Limits of Painting and Poetry.* Translation by E. A. McCormick. Baltimore.

Létoublon, F. 1995. Review of Nagy 1994c. *Revue de philologie* 68:285–290.

————, ed. 1997. *Hommage à Milman Parry: Le style formulaire de l'épopée et la théorie de l'oralité poétique.* Amsterdam.

Liddell, H. G., R. Scott, and H. Stuart Jones., eds. 1940. *Greek-English Lexicon.* 9th ed. Oxford.

Loraux, N., G. Nagy, and L. Slatkin, eds. 2001. *Antiquities.* Postwar French Thought, ed. R. Naddaff, vol. 3. New York.

Lord, A. B. 1953. "Homer's Originality: Oral Dictated Texts." *Transactions of the American Philological Association* 94:124–134.

————. 1960. *The Singer of Tales.* Harvard Studies in Comparative Literature 24. Cambridge, Mass. [2d ed., with introduction by S. Mitchell and G. Nagy (Cambridge, Mass., 2000).]

————. 1991. *Epic Singers and Oral Tradition.* Ithaca, N.Y.

————. 1995. *The Singer Resumes the Tale.* Edited by M. L. Lord. Ithaca, N.Y.

Louden, B. 2002. "Eurybates, Odysseus, and the Duals in Book 9 of the *Iliad.*" *Colby Quarterly* 38:62–76.

Lowenstam, S. 1993. *The Scepter and the Spear: Studies on Forms of Repetition in the Homeric Poems.* Lanham, Md.

————. 1997. "Talking Vases: The Relationship between the Homeric Poems and Archaic Representations of Epic Myth." *Transactions of the American Philological Association* 127:21–76.

Lynn-George, M. 1988. *Epos: Word, Narrative and the Iliad.* Atlantic Highlands, N.J.

Macleod, C., ed. 1982. *Homer Iliad Book XXIV.* Cambridge.

Marg, W. 1956. "Das erste Lied des Demodokos." In *Navicula Chiloniensis: Festschrift F. Jacoby,* 16–29. Leiden.

Martin, R. P. 1989. *The Language of Heroes: Speech and Performance in the Iliad.* Ithaca, N.Y.

————. 1993. "Telemachus and the Last Hero Song." *Colby Quarterly* 29:222–240.

———. 2000. "Wrapping Homer Up: Cohesion, Discourse, and Deviation in the *Iliad*." In A. Sharrock and H. Morales, eds., *Intratextuality: Greek and Roman Textual Relations*, 43–65. Oxford.

Meillet, A. 1925. *La méthode comparative en linguistique historique*. Paris.

Mitchell, S., and G. Nagy. 2000. Introduction to A. B. Lord, *The Singer of Tales*, 2d ed. Pp. vii–xxix. Cambridge, Mass.

Morris, I., and B. Powell, eds. 1997. *A New Companion to Homer*. Leiden.

Muellner, L. 1976. *The Meaning of Homeric* ΕΥΧΟΜΑΙ *through Its Formulas*. Innsbrucker Beiträge zur Sprachwissenschaft 13. Innsbruck.

———. 1996. *The Anger of Achilles: Mēnis in Greek Epic*. Ithaca, N.Y.

Murnaghan, S. 1987. *Disguise and Recognition in the* Odyssey. Princeton.

Murray, P., ed. 1996. *Plato on Poetry: Ion*, Republic *376e–398b*, Republic *595–608b*. With commentary. Cambridge.

Nagy, G. 1974. *Comparative Studies in Greek and Indic Meter*. Harvard Studies in Comparative Literature 33. Cambridge, Mass.

———. 1979. *The Best of the Achaeans: Concepts of the Hero in Archaic Greek Poetry*. Baltimore.

———. 1981. "An Evolutionary Model for the Text Fixation of the Homeric Epos." In Foley 1981:390–393.

———. 1990a. *Pindar's Homer: The Lyric Possession of an Epic Past*. Baltimore.

———. 1990b. *Greek Mythology and Poetics*. Ithaca, N.Y.

———. 1992a. "Homeric Questions." *Transactions of the American Philological Association* 122:17–60.

———. 1992b. "Mythological Exemplum in Homer." In R. Hexter and D. Selden, eds., *Innovations of Antiquity*, 311–331. New York and London.

———. 1992c. Introduction. In Homer, *The Iliad*, translated by R. Fitzgerald, Everyman's Library no. 60, v–xxi. New York.

———. 1994–1995. "Genre and Occasion." ΜΗΤΙΣ: *Revue d'anthropologie du monde grec ancien* 9–10:11–25.

———. 1994a. "The Name of Achilles: Questions of Etymology and 'Folk Etymology'." *Illinois Classical Studies* 19, Studies in Honor of Miroslav Marcovich 2:3–9.

———. 1994b. "The Name of Apollo: Etymology and Essence." In J. Solomon, ed., *Apollo: Origins and Influences*, 3–7. Tucson.

———. 1994c. *Le meilleur des Achéens: La fabrique du héros dans la poésie grecque archaïque*. Translated by J. Carlier and N. Loraux. Paris.

———. 1995a. "An Evolutionary Model for the Making of Homeric Poetry: Comparative Perspectives." In Carter and Morris 1995:163–179. Recast in Nagy 1996b.

———. 1995b. Review of Foley 1991. *Classical Journal* 91:93–94.

———. 1996a. *Poetry as Performance: Homer and Beyond*. Cambridge.

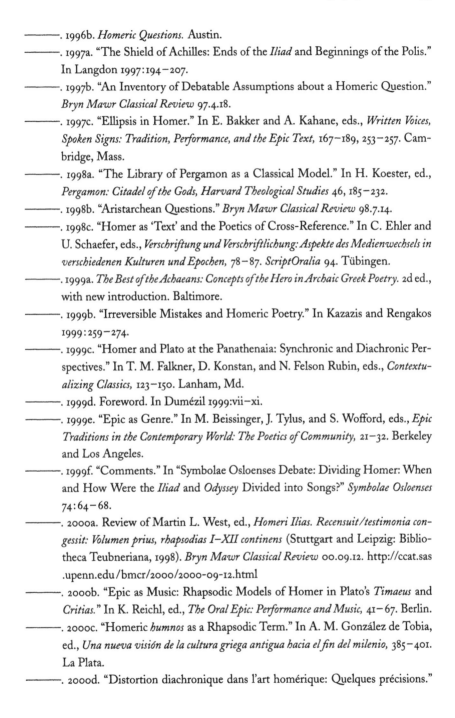

————. 1996b. *Homeric Questions.* Austin.

————. 1997a. "The Shield of Achilles: Ends of the *Iliad* and Beginnings of the Polis." In Langdon 1997:194–207.

————. 1997b. "An Inventory of Debatable Assumptions about a Homeric Question." *Bryn Mawr Classical Review* 97.4.18.

————. 1997c. "Ellipsis in Homer." In E. Bakker and A. Kahane, eds., *Written Voices, Spoken Signs: Tradition, Performance, and the Epic Text,* 167–189, 253–257. Cambridge, Mass.

————. 1998a. "The Library of Pergamon as a Classical Model." In H. Koester, ed., *Pergamon: Citadel of the Gods, Harvard Theological Studies* 46, 185–232.

————. 1998b. "Aristarchean Questions." *Bryn Mawr Classical Review* 98.7.14.

————. 1998c. "Homer as 'Text' and the Poetics of Cross-Reference." In C. Ehler and U. Schaefer, eds., *Verschriftung und Verschriftlichung: Aspekte des Medienwechsels in verschiedenen Kulturen und Epochen,* 78–87. *ScriptOralia* 94. Tübingen.

————. 1999a. *The Best of the Achaeans: Concepts of the Hero in Archaic Greek Poetry.* 2d ed., with new introduction. Baltimore.

————. 1999b. "Irreversible Mistakes and Homeric Poetry." In Kazazis and Rengakos 1999:259–274.

————. 1999c. "Homer and Plato at the Panathenaia: Synchronic and Diachronic Perspectives." In T. M. Falkner, D. Konstan, and N. Felson Rubin, eds., *Contextualizing Classics,* 123–150. Lanham, Md.

————. 1999d. Foreword. In Dumézil 1999:vii–xi.

————. 1999e. "Epic as Genre." In M. Beissinger, J. Tylus, and S. Wofford, eds., *Epic Traditions in the Contemporary World: The Poetics of Community,* 21–32. Berkeley and Los Angeles.

————. 1999f. "Comments." In "Symbolae Osloenses Debate: Dividing Homer: When and How Were the *Iliad* and *Odyssey* Divided into Songs?" *Symbolae Osloenses* 74:64–68.

————. 2000a. Review of Martin L. West, ed., *Homeri Ilias. Recensuit/testimonia congessit: Volumen prius, rhapsodias I–XII continens* (Stuttgart and Leipzig: Bibliotheca Teubneriana, 1998). *Bryn Mawr Classical Review* 00.09.12. http://ccat.sas.upenn.edu/bmcr/2000/2000-09-12.html

————. 2000b. "Epic as Music: Rhapsodic Models of Homer in Plato's *Timaeus* and *Critias.*" In K. Reichl, ed., *The Oral Epic: Performance and Music,* 41–67. Berlin.

————. 2000c. "Homeric *humnos* as a Rhapsodic Term." In A. M. González de Tobia, ed., *Una nueva visión de la cultura griega antigua hacia el fin del milenio,* 385–401. La Plata.

————. 2000d. "Distortion diachronique dans l'art homérique: Quelques précisions."

In C. Darbo-Peschanski, ed., *Constructions du temps dans le monde ancien*, 417–426. Paris.

———. 2001a. "Homeric Poetry and Problems of Multiformity: The 'Panathenaic Bottleneck.'" *Classical Philology* 96:109–119.

———. 2001b. "The Textualizing of Homer." In J. Helldén, M. S. Jensen, and T. Pettitt, eds., *Inclinate Aurem—Oral Perspectives on Early European Verbal Culture*, 57–84. Odense.

———. 2001c. "Reading Bakhtin Reading the Classics: An Epic Fate for Conveyors of the Heroic Past." In R. B. Branham, ed., *Bakhtin and the Classics*, 71–96. Evanston, Ill.

———. 2002a. *Plato's Rhapsody and Homer's Music: The Poetics of the Panathenaic Festival in Classical Athens*. Cambridge, Mass. and Athens.

———. 2002b. "The Language of Heroes as Mantic Poetry: Hypokrisis in Homer." In M. Reichel and A. Rengakos, eds., *Beiträge zur Homerforschung: Festschrift Wolfgang Kullmann*, 141–150. Stuttgart.

Oesterreicher, W. 1993. "*Verschriftung* und *Verschriftlichung* im Kontext medialer und konzeptioneller Schriftlichkeit." In U. Schaefer, ed., *Schriftlichkeit im frühen Mittelalter*, 267–292. Tübingen.

Olson, S. D. 1995. *"Blood and Iron": Stories and Storytelling in Homer's* Odyssey. Leiden.

Parry, A. 1966. "Have We Homer's *Iliad?*" *Yale Classical Studies* 20:177–216.

———, ed. 1971. *The Making of Homeric Verse: The Collected Papers of Milman Parry*. Oxford.

Parry, M. *See* A. Parry 1971 (abbreviated *MHV*).

Pelliccia, H. N. 1985. "The Structure of the Archaic Greek Hymns." Doctoral dissertation, Yale University.

Peradotto, J. 1990. *Man in the Middle Voice: Name and Narration in the* Odyssey. Princeton.

Perpillou, J.-L. 1970. Review of E. Benveniste, *Le vocabulaire des institutions indo-européennes*, 2 vols. (Paris, 1969). *Revue des études grecques* 83:534–537.

Pfeiffer, R. 1968. *History of Classical Scholarship: From the Beginnings to the End of the Hellenistic Age*. Oxford.

Porter, J. I. 1992. "Hermeneutic Lines and Circles: Aristarchus and Crates on the Exegesis of Homer." In R. Lamberton and J. J. Keaney, eds., *Homer's Ancient Readers: The Hermeneutics of Greek Epic's Earliest Exegetes*, 67–114. Princeton.

Powell, B. 1991. *Homer and the Origin of the Greek Alphabet*. Cambridge.

———. 1997. Review of Nagy 1996a. *Bryn Mawr Classical Review* 97.3.21.

Pucci, P. 1979. "The Song of the Sirens." *Arethusa* 12:121–132.

———. 1987. *Odysseus Polytropos: Intertextual Readings in the* Odyssey *and the* Iliad. Ithaca, N.Y.

———. 1995. Pucci 1987, 2d ed., with a new afterword at 247–258. Ithaca, N.Y.

Reichel, M. 1994. *Fernbeziehungen in der Ilias. ScriptOralia* no. 62. Tübingen.

Rengakos, A. 1993. *Der Homertext und die Hellenistischen Dichter.* Hermes Einzelschriften 64. Stuttgart.

Richards, I. A. 1936. *The Philosophy of Rhetoric.* Oxford.

Rüter, K. 1969. *Odysseeinterpretationen: Untersuchungen zum ersten Buch und zur Phaiakis.* Edited by K. Matthiessen. *Hypomnemata* no. 19. Göttingen.

Rutherford, R. B. 1991–1993. "From the *Iliad* to the *Odyssey.*" *Bulletin of the Institute of Classical Studies* 38:37–54.

Saussure, F. de. 1916. *Cours de linguistique générale.* Critical edition, 1972, by T. de Mauro. Paris.

Schrader, H., ed. 1890. *Quaestionum Homericarum ad Odysseam pertinentium reliquiae.* Leipzig.

Scully, S. 1990. *Homer and the Sacred City.* Ithaca, N.Y.

Seaford, R. 1994. *Reciprocity and Ritual: Homer and Tragedy in the Developing City-State.* Oxford.

Sherratt, E. S. 1990. "'Reading the Texts': Archaeology and the Homeric Question." *Antiquity* 64:807–824.

Stanley, K. 1993. *The Shield of Achilles: Narrative Structure in the Iliad.* Princeton.

Stansbury-O'Donnell, M. D. 1995. "Reading Pictorial Narrative: The Law Court Scene of the Shield of Achilles." In Carter and Morris 1995:315–334.

Svenbro, J. 1988. *Phrasikleia: Anthropologie de la lecture en Grèce ancienne.* Paris.

———. 1993. *Phrasikleia: An Anthropology of Reading.* Translation by J. Lloyd of Svenbro 1988. Ithaca, N.Y.

Taplin, O. 1980. "The Shield of Achilles within the *Iliad.*" *Greece and Rome* 27:1–21.

Van Wees, H. 2002. "Homer and Early Greece." *Colby Quarterly* 38:94–117.

Verdenius, W. J. 1972. "Notes on the Proem of Hesiod's *Theogony.*" *Mnemosyne* 25:225–260.

Volk, K. 2002. "ΚΛΕΟΣ ΑΦΘΙΤΟΝ Revisited." *Classical Philology* 97:61–68.

Watkins, C. 1995. *How to Kill a Dragon: Aspects of Indo-European Poetics.* New York.

West, M. L. 1981. "The Singing of Homer and the Modes of Early Greek Music." *Journal of Hellenic Studies* 101:113–129.

———. 1985. *The Hesiodic Catalogue of Women: Its Nature, Structure and Origins.* Oxford.

———. 1990. "Archaische Heldendichtung: Singen und Schreiben." In W. Kullmann and M. Reichel, eds., *Der Übergang von der Mündlichkeit zur Literatur bei den Griechen,* pp. 33–50. Tübingen.

Westbrook, R. 1992. "The Trial Scene in the *Iliad.*" *Harvard Studies in Classical Philology* 94:53–76.

Whitman, C. 1958. *Homer and the Heroic Tradition.* Cambridge, Mass.

Wilson, D. F. 1997. "The Politics of Compensation in the Homeric *Iliad.*" Ph.D. dissertation, University of Texas.

———. 2002. *Ransom, Revenge, and Heroic Identity in the* Iliad. Cambridge.

Wolff, H. J. 1946. "The Origin of Juridical Litigation among the Greeks." *Traditio* 4:31–87.

Index

Achilles, 12–13, 15–19, 25, 27, 38, 43–44, 50–55, 72–73, 78, 80–86; etymology of his name, 17; shield of, xi, 72–73, 77, 80, 86
Agamemnon, 13–14, 21, 54, 83–84
Aithiopis, 70
Ajax, 50–54, 81, 84
aksitaṣ (Vedic) 'unwilting, imperishable,' 48
ametakinēton 'unchangeable,' 31
anakrinein 'interrogate' and *anakrisis* 'interrogation,' 38
aoidē 'song,' 43
aoidos 'singer,' 6–7, 41–42
apangellein 'announce,' 32–34
aphthiton 'unwilting, imperishable,' 27, 46
apodeiknusthai 'perform,' 45
apoina 'ransom,' 55, 72, 80–81, 83–84
Apollo, 13–15, 18–19, 21
Aristarchus, x, 3, 50–51, 67, 69, 70
Aristotle
  Poetics: ix, 8, 37
  Politics: 37
  Rhetoric: 36
Athena, 58
Athenaeus, x
Athenians, 33–34
Athens, 2, 28, 34, 70
attributive and predicative adjectives, 27, 39, 47–48
audience, xi, xii, 9, 17, 22, 33, 40, 46, 59, 70–71, 75, 80, 85–86
Augenblickserfindung, 16
aulōidos 'aulode,' 42
author, concept of, ix, 9, 31, 66, 74

Bacchylides, 36
Briseis, 83–84

Calchas, 25–29
citharode. See *kitharōidos*
city-state, xi
clairvoyance, v, x, 21, 49
cledonomancy, 57, 59
composition (vs. performance). *See* performance
composition-in-performance, 6–7, 15–16, 23, 39–40, 44, 49–50, 69
Crates, 50–52
Croesus, 32–33
crystallization, 13
Cycle, epic, ix, 70
Cypria, 70
Cyrus, 32–33

dactylic hexameter, 34, 42, 44
Delphi, 14, 32–34
Demetrius of Phalerum, 2
Demodokos, 18–19, 42, 44, 54
dēmos/dāmos 'district,' 74–77, 79, 81
Demosthenes, 36
diachronic, 1–2, 9, 16, 19, 39–48, 83–84; definition of, 1; vs. historical, 1; vs. synchronic, 1–2, 16, 39–45, 48
diachronic skewing, 39–48
dianoia, meaning of, x
dictation: models of, 4–5, 67; theory of, 5, 50, 60, 64–66
Dieuchidas of Megara, 44
dikē 'judgment,' 74, 85
Diogenes Laertius (1.57), 43